The Last Farm on
CHAPPAQUIDDICK

Edo Potter

The Last Farm on
CHAPPAQUIDDICK
1932–1945

by Edo Potter

VINEYARD STORIES
Edgartown, Massachusetts

Volume Copyright ©2010 by Edo Potter

Published by Vineyard Stories
RR 1, Box 65-B9, Edgartown, MA 02539
508 221 2338
www.vineyardstories.com

Library of Congress Number: 2010924411
ISBN: 9780982714607

Second Printing, 2012

Editor: Jan Pogue, Vineyard Stories
Designer: Jill Dible, Atlanta, GA
Page six map: Dana Gaines

Printed in China

To my father, who started it all.

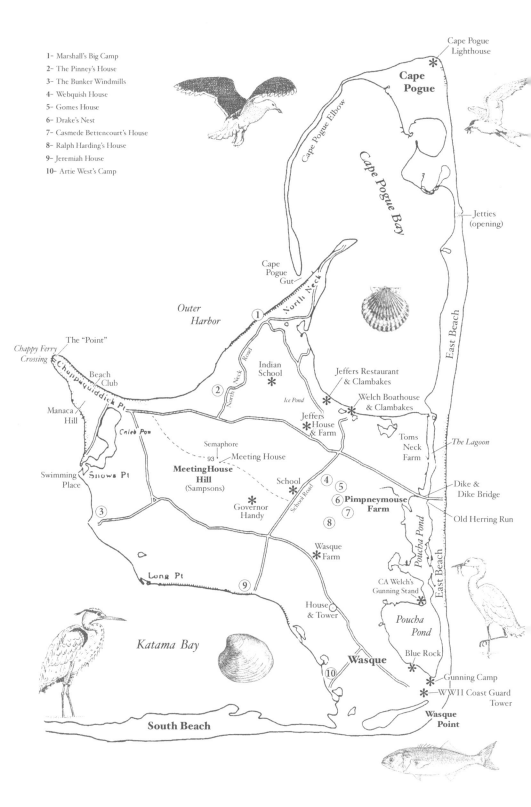

1- Marshall's Big Camp
2- The Pinney's House
3- The Bunker Windmills
4- Webquish House
5- Gomes House
6- Drake's Nest
7- Casmede Bettencourt's House
8- Ralph Harding's House
9- Jeremiah House
10- Artie West's Camp

Cape Pogue Lighthouse

Cape Pogue

Cape Pogue Elbow

Cape Pogue Bay

Jetties (opening)

East Beach

Outer Harbor

Cape Pogue Gut

North Neck

①

The "Point"

Chappy Ferry Crossing

Chappaquiddick Pt

Beach Club

②

North Neck Road

Indian School

Ice Pond

Jeffers Restaurant & Clambakes

Welch Boathouse & Clambakes

Jeffers House & Farm

Toms Neck Farm

The Lagoon

Manaca Hill

Caleb Pon

Semaphore
93
Meeting House

MeetingHouse Hill
(Sampsons)

School

④ ⑤

⑥ **Pimpneymouse Farm**

⑦

Dike & Dike Bridge

Swimming Place

Snows Pt

Governor Handy

⑧

Old Herring Run

③

Poucha Pond

Wasque Farm

Long Pt

⑨

House & Tower

CA Welch's Gunning Stand

Poucha Pond

East Beach

Katama Bay

Wasque

Blue Rock

⑩

Gunning Camp

WWII Coast Guard Tower

Wasque Point

South Beach

Table of Contents

Young Edo Potter on Laddie, helping Frank Drake cultivate corn.

Foreword

ICOLLECT THE PUBLISHED AUTOBIOGRAPHIES, DIARIES, oral histories, and personal legends of Island authors. Through them, I satisfy a longing to put myself on the ground of old Martha's Vineyard, to see the landscape as these writers once saw it, to embark with them on the boats they sailed and the seas they knew, to be with them for a moment while they did their work, tended to their families, traveled their roads, and met and spoke with their friends and neighbors along the way – in short, to have the Island as it once was come to life.

I've been waiting for the memoir you now hold in your hands for fourteen years. It's the story of an old friend, devoted public servant, driven sailboat racer, and offshore farmer – well, to be more specific about this, offshore-offshore farmer, given that the farm she has worked with three generations of her family lies on the island of Chappaquiddick, which lies separated physically and spiritually in every possible way from the main Island of Martha's Vineyard, only six hundred feet across a tideswept harbor entrance.

The first time I realized that Edo Potter might write a book about her lifetime of living and farming on Chappaquiddick — a family story that reaches back nearly eighty years and continues even now — was in the spring of 1996, when Edo, with customary diffidence, first mentioned the idea of it to me.

I was interviewing Edo for a magazine story about the young women who had grown up racing sailboats on Vineyard waters in the middle years of the twentieth century. This was a time when boys and girls rarely competed against one another in any sport, and the record showed that these particular young ladies — with what many anecdotes suggested was a nearly merciless level of competitiveness — had gone out there summer after summer and just plain thrashed the lads on their way to a host of regional and even national championships.

I knew Edo to be a gentlewoman who would never take credit for anything if there were even a chance that she could plausibly deflect it to someone else. But I also knew that she had been one of the young ladies out on those racecourses, ripping the hearts out of the hapless sailor boys and snaring titles of her own.

As we spoke, she was pulling up memories of her racing days from the first few pages of what would become this book, and when she asked, hesitantly, whether I thought the story of her life on Pimpneymouse Farm might one day make a modest but worthwhile memoir, I briefly thought about ditching the racing story altogether and pitching hers to my editor instead. But I also knew I'd have to give the story up, for even a brief review of those few pages at her dining room table proved to me that no one could ever tell Edo Potter's story quite the way she could.

My family has known the Potters for more than forty years. In 1975, Edo and my stepfather brought the first Herreshoff 12-1/2 sloops to Edgartown; today our boats lie at nearly adjacent moorings, two among more than sixty that now tack across harbor waters nearly every summer's day under tan, gaff-rigged mainsails. (I've followed my stepfather's tradition of crossing finish lines astern of Edo for three cheerfully frustrating decades.) And my sister pastured Gaigyn, her Arabian gelding, at the Potters' for nearly twenty years. "It meant a lot to me that he could live out his days happily on Chappy at Pimpneymouse Farm," she tells me now.

And it means a lot to me that this book is finally here. Edo Potter – former four-term Edgartown selectman, award-winning conservationist, world traveler, competitor, farmer, and friend – knows the Vineyard as well as anyone I know, and Chappy better than most any of us know. As I look at my library of Vineyard memoirs, I see that Edo's will stand alphabetically between one written by a West Tisbury farmer and another by a part-time rumrunner. The gentlewoman I've known all these years, on land and on water, will take a great deal of pleasure from that.

Tom Dunlop
EDGARTOWN

The entrance sign for Pimpneymouse, still located on the main road through Chappaquiddick.

PARADISE

*"For many, many years Chappaquiddick Island had
complete tranquility, beautiful lonely beaches, broad fields,
and practically deserted sandy roads. Only a few hardy
families lived there all year round, and during the summer
several dozen or more families joined them to enjoy the
solitude and beauty of a rather primitive island paradise."*

—WALTER WILLIAMSON, *LOW ON THE FAMILY TREE*

NO ONE TOLD ME WE WERE LIVING ON A PRIMITIVE
island, but we surely knew it was paradise.

An almost eighty-year, multigenerational perspective
has made me appreciate what an extraordinary place
Chappaquiddick was in the years between 1932 and 1945,
when I was growing up on Pimpneymouse Farm, my
family's island home. These dates reflect the time between
the first visit to "Chappy" by our whole family and the

final summer before my going off to college. They were years when Pimpneymouse was one of four working farms on the little island. Now it is the last one left.

I was five years old on my first visit to Chappaquiddick in the winter of 1932, and I don't remember much of Chappy except for the extreme cold. On that first trip, we spent time during the day at my father's Gunning Stand (a hunting camp) on Poucha Pond, and the night in the old farmhouse where I still live seventy-eight years later and which then had very little heat and no electricity, running water, or telephone.

My father bought our hundred-acre farm on Chappy in 1928 because he was keenly interested in the duck and goose hunting provided by the pond. When he gave up hunting, he turned his attention to the backland, away from the pond. It hadn't been farmed for years but still had open fields and good soils. My father had had an abiding interest in farming ever since his mother allowed him to bring up chickens in her big Victorian bathtub in their house in Boston.

His move from hunter to farmer marked the beginning of Pimpneymouse Farm. As we began spending long summers on the island, he built farm buildings and chicken

The road to Charlie Welch's Gunning Camp, long before trees populated the island.

houses and coops, plowed the fields, and created an orchard and vegetable garden. Ben Pease, a year-rounder and native whose family had lived on Chappy for a long time, told my father that the original name of the farm was "Pimpneymouse Farm," and that Pimpney was Indian for "little." Since there were a lot of little mice around, my father believed him and asked a friend who was a commercial artist to make the magnificent sign that has hung over the barn for seventy-five years. When Pease saw the sign, he laughed and said, "You didn't believe me, did you?"

But the name stuck.

I WAS THE MIDDLE OF THREE SISTERS, AND MY PARENTS brought us for that first trip from our home in Marblehead, which in the early 1930s was a tiny fishing village. Most of the houses in Marblehead were small and close together, the streets narrow and winding. The only freedom for my sisters and me was roller-skating on the sidewalks. On our first visit to Chappaquiddick, even as young as I was, I remember sensing how wide open the island was, and the potential there for freedom. I yearned to come back in warmer weather and explore.

And then, just like that, we found ourselves in May 1933 on the ferry *Nobska*, crossing Vineyard Sound to Martha's Vineyard, then driving across the big island to the Edgartown landing for the launch *Sleepy*. Built and captained by Tony Bettencourt, *Sleepy* towed a homemade scow that Tony had built to carry cars and livestock to Chappaquiddick.

Here was a place where we were free to roam the grasslands and sheep-grazed fields, over rolling hills much more apparent than they are now. It was the start of my lifelong love and fascination for Pimpneymouse Farm and Chappaquiddick, the place where my husband, Robert, and I have raised our four children, and where every building, field, and woodland on the farm has a place in my own history and the history of the island.

The longevity of the farm's ownership is unusual. It preserves a continuity of memories that I want to capture in writing before it is too late, to help to explain to those who arrive today why the island's past has such resonance for its future. Chappy and Pimpneymouse Farm still provide the fourth generation the same joy and pleasure, the same excitement and enjoyment and even solace as it did long ago in the 1930s and 1940s.

My father always said he believed that Chappaquiddick would be slower to develop than the rest of the Vineyard, and, he added, "When it gets built up, I will move to Nova Scotia."

We never moved to Nova Scotia.

Edo on Lucille with her dog Trixie,
on a beach few people visited.

Chapter One

THE SEPARATED ISLAND

CHAPPAQUIDDICK IS A 3,700-ACRE ISLAND OFF THE EAST side of the "big island" of Martha's Vineyard. A microcosm of the larger island, Chappy, as it is known locally, has the same diverse geology as the Vineyard and is something of a marvel, with formations that have fascinated more than one scientist and naturalist: The north shore is high with dramatic contours – deep hollows called kettle holes and high ridges officially called "eskers." The southern and eastern shores are outwash plains formed by the glacier that covered the entire island thousands of years ago.

The highest point on Chappaquiddick – and, in fact, the highest point in all of Edgartown, the village on the Vineyard to which Chappy is legally attached – is Sampson's Hill at ninety-three feet. It is often called Meeting House Hill because of the small church at its summit in the 1920s and early 1930s. A ridge runs north and south across the top of the hill crowned by huge glacial erratics (boulders) that are rare on Chappaquiddick.

Until the "Great Gale" of 1723 closed off the east end of Poucha Pond from the Atlantic Ocean, Chappaquiddick was actually three islands. Cape Pogue was an entirely separate island stretching from Little Neck to the Gut, creating what's now called Cape Pogue Pond. Another small island lay just off the present East Beach.

When the white men arrived on the Vineyard and then Chappy in the mid-1600s, they found a barren landscape kept open by the Wampanoag Native Americans by felling trees and burning. The Wampanoags themselves had lived on Chappy for over 9,000 years, according to carbon-dated arrowheads found on the farm and now housed in the Martha's Vineyard Museum. The tribe migrated to the island during the glacial age, when they simply walked from Cape Cod or even Georges Bank on dry land that later became water when the glaciers melted.

FROM THE BEGINNING, CHAPPAQUIDDICK SHARED LITTLE IN common with its nearest neighbor. While Edgartown became a bustling whaling village, Chappy remained rural and savagely beautiful in its austere loneliness. Its only tentative connection to Edgartown and the main island was a barrier beach at the southern end of Katama Bay, a connection that routinely disappeared through the centuries and completely disappeared again in April 2007 during a northeast storm.

But if they didn't want to live there, Edgartown citizens took advantage of the open, grassy landscape and brought their animals over to Chappy in early October via the "Swimming Place," the narrowest part of Katama Bay where it joins Edgartown Harbor. Some people walked or led their livestock along the beach between the two islands, or put small animals in sturdy rowboats for the trip across. The animals were pastured there until spring, when they returned to Edgartown. No fences or shepherds were needed, since the animals would not cross the water without strong urging. Before returning to Edgartown in April, the sheep were herded to Cape Pogue to be sheared in Shear Pen Pond, which still carries that name.

Empty and barren, the island was an inconvenient place to get to, and only hardy families could survive there. Prior to the first motorized ferry in 1934, there were only rowboats for transportation and a launch that towed a small scow. The few year-round people lived in the center of the island away from the gale force winds and writhing seas of winter. They made a living tending their sheep, growing their own food, and living off the land and the bounty of the sea.

Yet none of this – not geological formations nor vistas nor winter gales – meant much to me when I first came to Chappy. All I knew was the wide-open land, the empty beaches with no footprints except ours, and an island small enough so that everyone knew each other. The year-round residents provided food and seafood to the summer people, bringing ice and other necessities by rowboat, sometimes towing a flat wooden scow to transport livestock and horses for the buggies left here year round by the summer people.

I could feel the power of the island even from a young age during the four months of our summers there, the feelings that eventually led me to claim Pimpneymouse as my year-round home. Standing on top of Meeting House Hill, I could see 360 degrees, virtually the entire island and much of the south shore of the Vineyard. The ocean, ponds, and streams were full of fish, eels, crabs, and shellfish. Wasque, which has been kept open for centuries by man's effort, was awash in blueberries during the summer, beach plums during the early fall, and other treasures the rest of the year, gifts

from both land and sea. All of this was encircled by white sand beaches and wonderful blue waters.

The wonder of it has lasted me almost eighty years.

BY 1928, WHEN MY FATHER FIRST CAME TO CHAPPAQUIDDICK, there were a few summer people who had bought land, often from the Wampanoags, and built a handful of houses along North Neck and Katama Bay. Most people, though,

A view from Meneca Hill on Chappy toward the Edgartown Lighthouse. Early Beach Club buildings are on the outer harbor.

simply viewed our Chappy as "nothing but a godforsaken sand dune," as one described it.

My father, called "Charlie" by most of his friends, relished the isolation and the simplicity of living here, the closeness of the community, and all the opportunities that Chappy offered. He, like many others before him, had bought the land for hunting. Duck and goose hunting was popular during this time, and many hunting camps existed on the Vineyard in the 1920s and 1930s. Chappy itself had three hunting camps: two on Poucha Pond, including my father's and one at Wasque owned by Curtis Nye Smith; and one on Cape Pogue Pond owned by Charles Simpson.

Charlie Welch with his three daughters outside the farm barn, and a clipping from the Vineyard Gazette.

It was mostly a man's sport, and women and children were not included. However, in 1932 my father, who was on Chappy hunting and tending to his live geese decoys, invited us down for Thanksgiving so that he didn't have to leave the island to return to Marblehead. It was cold, empty, and almost unpopulated on Chappy, and my mother, myself, and my two sisters had to get across from Edgartown aboard a small launch called *Sleepy*, captained by Tony Bettencourt. We must have thought we were at the end of the world.

OUR FIRST LONG VISIT, WHEN MY SISTERS AND I WERE FOUR, six, and eight years old, came to be a traditional journey every summer. I remember the flurry of preparations before we left Marblehead, then the drive from Marblehead to Woods Hole that took all day. Our Chevrolet sedan was packed to the rooftop, not only with two adults and three children but a cage of white mice and two canaries belonging to my sister Ruth. One summer my sister's canary had babies. We thought it was a wonderful occasion until we discovered they were too young to travel, and we had to delay our departure. Every year trunks and suitcases were shipped via "Railway Express," the precursor to United Parcel Service and Federal Express.

The trip through Boston, Taunton, and Buzzards Bay seemed endless. No reservations were needed on the steamers that took us to the Vineyard. We just arrived at the dock and waited for the next boat. Sometimes the wait was two to three hours because the steamer from Woods Hole went all the way to Nantucket and back. During the wait, we got out of the car and explored the dock and Sam Cahoon's Fishmarket next door.

When the steamer arrived it sounded its unique steam whistle, a welcoming sound with a more melodious, higher, sweeter pitch than the boats of today. It came along the front of the dock, then warped itself around the corner of the dock where the ferries come in today, using the huge bollards at the corner as a turning point. (Bollards are large spiles that hold the dock firmly when a big boat has to make a ninety-degree turn.)

Once settled in the slip, stern first, a large side door near the boat's bow opened into the car deck. A heavy ramp was manhandled up to the opening. Passengers had to get out and go aboard at the stern while the cars were driven on board.

The three Welch sisters the first year they spent the summer on Chappy.

Frank Drake

OUR STORYTELLER

F rank Drake came to work for my father in 1928 and continued working for him for seventeen years. He was in charge of the garden and drove the small fire-engine-red delivery truck filled with vegetables, fruit, milk, chickens, and eggs to the summer houses on Chappy.

Frank was a jack of all trades, good on boats, good in the gunning stand, good with horses, good in the garden, good with the hay crop, and good in the kitchen.

Since we three sisters were expected to do our share of hoeing with Frank in the nine-acre corn and potato fields, we heard all his stories. We were transfixed by the tales of all the things he had done in his lifetime — running a trolley in Boston, serving as a chef in a restaurant, crewing on a fishing boat, and accomplishing many unusual things. One of my sisters once speculated that Frank would have to be over one hundred years old to have done all the jobs he said he had.

Frank often used the rain of a thunderstorm to take a shower under the downspout from the rain gutter. This night the thunder and lightning accompanying the rain seemed more severe than usual. The next morning, he told us he had been struck by a lightning bolt that hit the ground about twenty-five-yards away. He said he was knocked flat and didn't come to for a long time.

We never could figure out whether this was true since he didn't look any the worse for the experience.

My sisters and I ran up to the top deck and leaned over the rail to be sure our loaded car made it on board safely. The driver drove the car straight on, across the freight deck, then "backed and filled" (as my father called it) many times between the stanchions on the freight deck in order to turn ninety degrees in a small space and drive toward the stern to the appropriate parking place.

Nobska was my favorite steamer. Passengers came in on the stern's side, and to the right was a grand staircase, wide and gracious with polished mahogany hand rails going up to the next deck. There was an elegant lunch counter, always clean and bright. A polished brass rail encircled the counter so that nothing could slip off in rough seas or when the ship rolled. The tables had white tablecloths, and the chairs were dark mahogany armchairs, polished by use.

Along the outside of the interior second deck were staterooms, used mostly by people on the three-hour trip to Nantucket after the Vineyard passengers were dropped off in Oak Bluffs. A woman named Mrs. Trent cared for the staterooms, and her husband was also employed by the boat line. Mr. and Mrs. Trent had a month's vacation in February when one of the steamers was in drydock for repairs and painting. They spent their vacation in their tiny house across the Chappy Road from Pimpneymouse Farm's biggest field. It has always been known as the Trent Field, named after them.

Once on the Vineyard, our vacation began, and we could hardly sit still long enough to get to the Chappy ferry. Our glorious, four-month summer was at hand.

For a time we were simply summer people, among the few who came to this spit of land between Edgartown and the Atlantic Ocean.

We felt like pioneers, with no electricity, telephone, or running water, and ready for any adventure.

Ruth, Hope, and Edo on the porch of "Lion's Hotel," their playhouse.

Ruth Y. Welch and Charles A. Welch,
pictured in 1924.

Chapter Two

THE END OF CITY LIFE

IT WAS, BY ALL STANDARDS, A STRANGE PLACE FOR US to be.

My father and mother, Ruth Yerxa Welch, were proper Bostonians whose parents owned prosperous businesses. My father had tried working in Boston at the family investment firm of Welch and Forbes, begun by his grandfather. He didn't like it, although I heard he was very successful. The story goes that my father was particularly good with older clients and often had the job of funeral arrangements and burial plans. This is why he called one of his racing boats *Undertaker*; he bought it with his fee for settling an estate.

My father's square brick house on Deerfield Street in Boston sat right on the edge of the Charles River, and is still there today. No Storrow Drive existed then, so the river lapped the side of his house. In the early 1900s, steps ran down the side of the wall behind the house to a small dock where my grandfather kept a launch. His boatman took him to work by water in the morning from Deerfield Street to downtown Boston and picked him up at night. Away from the water, a big lawn and garden behind a wrought-iron fence also remain today.

My mother was raised at 300 Marlboro Street in Boston, around the corner from Deerfield Street. She and her brother, John Yerxa, lived with their family in a brick row house. It was narrow and dark with windows only in the front and back. My mother was a beautiful young woman, warm and loving and full of fun. I remember a teenage cousin, Barbara Welch, saying to me, "I fell in love with your mother when I saw her in a white fur hat, being helped into a sleigh by your father, who drove her off into the snow-covered fields of Sugar Hill, New Hampshire."

Charlie and Ruth were not only neighbors but were also friends and went to the same dancing school in Boston, Miss Southers. Both families spent time in Marblehead in the summers, and both were keen on sailing and racing.

They married in 1922 in a traditional and formal wedding in one of Boston's largest churches, Trinity Church in Copley Square.

Although born and raised in Boston, both our parents agreed they did not want to live in the city. They moved to Marblehead after living a short time in a basement apartment on Beach Hill. That apartment was on the side of the hill with one side on street level and the back side opening into a small garden. My mother told the story of a cat

Henry D. Yerxa

A CHURCHGOING MAN

Henry D. Yerxa, my mother's grandfather, started the then-well-known Boston grocery store Cobb, Bates, and Yerxa. He was one of fifteen children born and brought up on a farm in New Brunswick, Canada.

In about 1850, when he was 18, he persuaded his father to let him go to Maine to help move cows to Massachusetts for sale. Henry was promised $1.50 a day to move the 128 head of cattle. He walked sixteen to eighteen miles a day and arrived in Brighton, where he had to load the cows onto a train to Boston — although he'd never seen a train or a cattle car.

Henry was paid $27 for the trip but found Boston too expensive to afford a room and food. He offered to work for C. D. Cobb, who owned a grocery store, but was turned down. Cobb did allow Henry to sleep in the back room. The next Saturday afternoon, business was "rushing," and Cobb asked Henry to help. Henry was so useful that Cobb kept him on and paid him $32 at the end of four weeks. Cobb then hired him full-time on the condition that Henry attend church and Sunday school every week. Cobb eventually turned the store over to Henry.

Ruth Welch, who was a highly regarded sailor, cruising on Roaring Bessie, *which she captained with an all-female crew.*

coming through the cellarlike front window and eating her parrot. That did it: the end of city life.

Marblehead in those days was just a little fishing village in the winter, although a busy and popular summer and sailing resort in the summer – a far cry from Chappaquiddick. Both my mother and father sailed and had done so since they were young. My mother's family had a summer house at the far end of the causeway between the main part of Marblehead and Marblehead Neck, a spit of rocky land and shoreline that protected Marblehead Harbor from storms and the Atlantic Ocean. My father's family spent summers and sailed in Nahant, south of Boston.

Marblehead Harbor was one of the major sailing spots, known worldwide. It had three yacht clubs and three boatyards that attracted large schooners, sleek racing boats, and fishing and work boats. I can remember the fishermen and workmen starting up their engines early in the morning, making the unique sound of "putt, putt, putt," a "one-lung engine" sound you never hear anymore.

Both my parents were adept sailors. My father became a successful international racing captain who competed all over the world. My mother was equally at home on the water, and though they never competed against each other, there was always a question about who was the best captain.

In Marblehead my father became friends with L. Francis Herreshoff, who designed many boats for him, from a kayak to a six-meter racing sailboat, from a motor sailer called *Walrus* to a fast, sleek fishing boat called *Gadget*. No one-design classes existed in the 1920s. Each boat that raced was individually designed and had to be within a certain set of parameters; the races were a competition between designers as well as skippers. Mr. Herreshoff was the son of the famous designer Nathanael Herreshoff of Bristol, Rhode Island, but didn't want to go into the family firm. He had rather "modern" ideas and wanted to design boats his own way and not according to tradition – certainly a sentiment my father could understand.

MY FATHER LIVED HIS LIFE INTENSELY AND SHIFTED FROM one interest to another, often precipitously. After years of passionate hunting and sailing he turned to farming and fishing. When his summer sailboats were stored away, my father turned his thoughts from sailing to hunting. When he bought the 100 acres of land on Chappy, he bought property that extended from the west side of the long field, at the Dike Road sharp corner in the now paved road, all the way to Poucha Pond as a place where he could hunt without worry of being overtaken by development – an issue even as early as the 1930s on Martha's Vineyard.

Although he ended up buying the entire farm he later named Pimpneymouse, he really wanted waterfront, again not so different from today's buyers. The land he purchased from Arthur R. Sharpe of New Bedford for his hunting camp included a gunning stand, a tower where the gunners sat waiting for the geese and ducks to fly in, following the live decoys that were released from a pen, also controlled from the tower.

Charles A. Welch, age 13, with his mother, Edith Thayer Welch.

Other than the tower, the camp consisted of two rooms: a bunkroom and an all-purpose kitchen, dining, and living area.

The land that came with the hunting camp had been farmed years before by the year-round Viera family. However, it had lain fallow for a number of years while Mr. Sharpe enthusiastically hunted waterfowl.

After my father bought the land in 1928, he visited the land sporadically until we spent our first summer in the Farm House in 1933. By then, my father had given up duck hunting after the federal government banned live decoys and put limits on the number of birds that could be shot.

Poucha Pond Fish and Meadow Company was a thriving business that sent fish far off island.

His old interest in farming resurfaced.

The land was still fertile and clear except for a few cedars that began to appear. The first summer he brought his family to stay on Chappy, my father started building farm structures, plowed up the old fields with a newly acquired workhorse, and created an orchard and a large vegetable garden.

My heavyset, strong father – proper Bostonian, international sailor, former businessman – was now a farmer.

Frank Drake and Lucille mowing the dry marsh on Poucha Pond.

Chapter Three

CHARLIE STARTS FARMING

DURING THE YEARS OF MY CHILDHOOD, PIMPNEYMOUSE Farm was a true working farm, called a "truck garden." My father loved farming, took it seriously, and threw himself into it, working alongside two very able people, Frank Drake and Ralph Harding. With the help of his three daughters, my father produced milk, cream, eggs, chickens for the table, vegetables from a large garden, and fruit from his orchard.

Chappaquiddick had a small summer colony in the 1930s who appreciated home delivery and fresh food. Frank made the deliveries door-to-door in a bright red truck with "Pimpneymouse Farm" emblazoned in white letters on the black sideboards. He also picked up orders for his next trip.

The Vieras, most of whom have moved to the New Bedford area, had farmed on a small scale before my father bought the land. Theirs was more of a subsistence farm, their "Home Place." The land was transformed under my father's guidance, although his work on the farm included far more than just growing things and milking cows. Besides the Farm House, many small outbuildings were scattered around. Most of them were in need of major repair, and some were torn down.

The first new structure that he built was a sturdy garage/ workshop in 1932, the beginning of a large barn. Tractors and trucks could be driven inside for repair, out of the rain and cold. The next section of the barn was built to house the equipment my father was acquiring and was the perfect place for mounting our new farm sign. Finally the horse barn and cow barn were added with the big loft above.

Today our hay is tied in bales, but in the 1930s the hay was brought in loose from the fields and pitched by pitch-forks from the big black truck into the barn by Ralph and Frank. The hay was pushed back into the loft by a gang of kids whom we were able to cajole into helping us. To avoid any possibility of spontaneous combustion, a common cause of barn fires in the days before mechanized baling, rock salt was spread on the hay, on top of each layer, until the barn was full to capacity. It was hard work, hot and sweaty, but when the fields were emptied of their hay and the barn was full of the sweet-smelling contents, the work became rewarding.

A round brooder house was added in the front of the barn for baby chicks, who were warmed by a kerosene burner. My father would go out at night to check on the brooder stove, to be sure that it wouldn't shut off during the night or, worse, get overheated with the disastrous result of dead chicks or even a fire.

Edo and Hope in the pony cart pulled by Cozy. The pony was a gift from a nearby family.

My father's hunting dogs, Chesapeake Bay retrievers, were housed in a small building near the edge of the woods, beyond the present harness house. Although friendly with the family, the dogs were leery of strangers and very protective. Trixie, the runt of the litter, was kept as a pet. She loved us and we loved her, and she followed us around like a shadow.

THE PIGPEN WAS ANOTHER IMPORTANT ADDITION. ORIG-inally it was a large open cement pen that housed pigs and piglets. They rooted and snuffled around in the manure that was dumped in every day along with the garbage from the house. Later my father built a shiny corrugated aluminum

A photo of the newly finished barn in 1938.

roof to provide protection for the pigs in the winter. For some unknown reason, my father called all the sows Mrs. Dennis. He liked to name his farm animals, but this practice made it harder to slaughter them and put their meat on the table, especially since my father delighted in exclaiming, "This is Mrs. Dennis that we are eating tonight."

The Milk House, still called by the same name, was where the milk from our four cows was separated from the cream and bottled. A shiny machine, turned by hand with a crank, made a comfortable humming sound. We children were not allowed into the building to see how it worked because it was necessary to keep everything clean and sterile. However, I remember the rhythmic whirring of the separator that went on and on and the thick cream that eventually appeared. The cream was so thick it wouldn't pour and was spooned out of the top of the bottle.

The final building near the barn was the Carriage House, painted green and with large white sliding doors. Its original purpose was to house the horse-drawn carriage and the horse-drawn farm equipment. Today it is jam-packed with motorized machinery. Although there is not a carriage in sight, this building is still called the Carriage House. The carriages sit in the covered pigpen today, since there are no more pigs housed there.

Chickens came next, lots of them. Housed in the round brooder house at first, the chickens were transferred when they were big enough into the long white chicken house, still standing near the vegetable garden. The chicken house had separate rooms, each holding lots of pullets (half-grown hens).

Large square metal boxes that held six dozen eggs were mailed to my grandmother in Boston on a regular schedule through the U.S. Postal Service. She liked fresh eggs and as long as she was alive, my father sent her eggs through the mail every week. They arrived overnight and unbroken. Even more astonishing, my father sent a large bouquet of sweet peas, my grandmother's favorite flowers, on the steamer for his mother's chauffeur to pick up in Woods Hole and drive them back to her in Boston.

SOMETIMES THE HENS WOULD PECK EACH OTHER CRUELLY, and the solution was to cut off a part of the top beak. This stopped the pecking but made it harder for the hen to eat.

Charlie Welch with a prize banty hen, a White Crested Black Polish.

As an alternative, the hens were fitted with a little pair of red glasses on their beak so they couldn't see well enough to peck. Marion Harding, Ralph's daughter, came to the farm at night with her father to help him put on the red glasses, since the hens were easier to catch at night and didn't squawk as much as in the daytime. I wish I had a picture of the hens in their glasses. It was funny to see them running around with little red glasses on their beaks.

Chickens and other fowl were favorites of my father. As my father developed the farm, he collected bantam chickens and built four more small chicken houses. One of them is still in use as a laying hens' house, next to the big barn.

My father's next project was a larger and longer bantam house that he built near the pine woodpile. It had enough headroom so a person could stand upright. Eight individual

$\mathcal{N}ature$
ON HER BEST BEHAVIOR

Mosquitoes and ticks – now both biting menaces – were once absent from Chappy. During the Depression, the federal government paid to have ditches dug in the salt marsh to drain the wet areas where mosquitoes breed. When the Town of Edgartown quit digging the ditches, the mosquitoes proliferated.

Ticks found their way to Chappy when summer people brought them on their dogs, or they may have arrived with the white-tailed deer that swam over to the Vineyard from the Elizabeth Islands in recent years.

Although skunks and raccoons were nonexistent, snakes were much more common. Huge black snakes liked to climb trees and lie along a branch, looking menacing. Riding under a tree and seeing a snake three feet long and as big around as my wrist was scary, although they were harmless and in fact were helpful since they ate rodents. My son Stephen had a pet snake he took to bed with him. The snake liked the warmth under the covers. I drew the line when the snake slithered out of his pajama top just as I bent down to kiss him goodnight. The snake had to stay in his tank after that.

rooms were separated with wire doors. This chicken house wasn't as large as his long layers house, and the eight "rooms" were each only about four feet square. A little door at floor level allowed the birds to go outdoors into separate wire pens and onto the grass.

His favorite bantams, such as White Crested Black Polish, Buff Cochins, and for a while, gamecocks, lived here. I enjoyed feeding and watering them. Entering the building at one end, I took them water and corn while being careful to keep them separate. Some of the pens held a couple of hens and their brood of baby chicks, but the gamecocks were always in individual pens. They were aggressive to each other but were always glad to see me bringing food and water.

Another of my father's interests was beekeeping. He set up hives in the apple and pear orchard and in the fall would bring the honeycombs into the house, put them in a huge

A haying day took much help: Frank Drake, on top of the hay; and from left Ralph Harding, pitching up hay; and Casmede Bettencourt, an unknown friend, Hope, and Edo.

"Mrs. Dennis" and Babe, the girls' favorite pony.

kettle on the hot stove and rotate them with a hand crank until they gave up their honey. It had to be very warm to separate the honey, so both burners in the black stove were on, and the windows shut to build up the heat. It was incredibly hot in the kitchen, but the outcome was delicious. One jar has been saved in the cellar since the 1930s. If historical reports are true, honey found in the tombs of the Pharaohs in Egypt is still good. Though I can't bear to open this last jar of our honey, I hope someday, someone will open it and prove that our honey, too, keeps indefinitely.

MY FATHER FARMED WITH HORSES FOR ABOUT FOUR YEARS but finally bought a tractor. It was a Cletrac with big metal caterpillar treads instead of wheels and tires. He thought it could do anything, but because the soil in the fields was sandy and soft, the tractor sank into the sand and became thoroughly stuck in the North Horse Pasture. It took two workhorses, a truck, and several men with shovels to extricate it. Afterward, my father used the tractor to cut firewood, mow the fields, and do many other farm chores.

The first vegetable garden was where firewood is now stored. During World War II, summer people couldn't come to Chappy because gas was rationed. Since my father couldn't sell his vegetables, fruit, chickens, eggs, and milk, he went looking for a new market. He asked the University of Massachusetts School of Agriculture what Chappaquid-

The newly finished barn (right) and an old chicken brooder house and storage shed.

dick's soil and climate were most suitable for and what kind of a crop could be sold all at once, instead of daily. The answer was potatoes.

Potatoes, potatoes, potatoes were planted everywhere, and although they took less cultivating than a mixture of vegetables, they needed to be hoed. I remember the rows of potatoes in the north and south horse pasture that was all one big nine-acre field. Hoeing one row seemed to take all day. The potatoes were all harvested at one time in the fall and were sold to the Navy's chef at the new big airport in the middle of the Vineyard.

Bob Potter, my future husband, arrived on Chappy on a bicycle in the early 1940s. He had persuaded a friend to go

on a bike trip with him and then deserted the friend to explore this place his aunt and uncle, Louie and Sally Howland, had described to him. The Howlands were great friends of my parents and had visited Chappy often. Bob made his way to the farm after dark, and he slept on the beach so he wouldn't awaken us. The second time he came for a visit, again after dark, he slept in the hay mow.

He was persuaded to help in the potato hoeing, the work perhaps mitigated by the three girls who worked alongside him. Later, my father rewarded Bob's hard work by taking him fishing on his boat, *Gadget,* in the Wasque Rips.

There was always pleasure mixed into the work. We three sisters did our share of what seemed to us backbreaking work. However, we were rewarded by getting off early to go riding,

Frank Drake's delivery truck went all over the island with fresh foods for the summer residents.

Ralph Harding
THE PIED PIPER

Ralph Harding was young and strong and skinny when he came to the farm in 1930 to help my father with the farming. He stayed sixty-three years.

Ralph loved children, and they responded to him. My mother called him the "Pied Piper" because he would walk from the barn to the chicken house with a string of children in diminishing sizes stretching out behind him. They wanted to "help" him do the chores. He was incredibly patient with us and taught us a great deal about the natural world and how to live off the land.

He taught us to hunt and shoot. And he taught us what it meant to make do. When things were lean for him, he trapped muskrats and even otters and sold their pelts to make ends meet. When Ralph found a silk parachute at Wasque during World War II, he brought it home, and his wife used the material for clothing. He kept an eye on us at all times; a barking dog or a strange light would bring him to the Farm House to check on it. There was a lone tree between his house and ours; when a hurricane took the tree down, he said he felt as if he'd lost an old friend.

When my father died in 1945, Frank Drake retired and Ralph was on his own on the farm. My mother spent the winters in Boston. Ralph held the farm together and helped my mother change it from a farm to a summer place. He kept the farm running until the children came back and helped out.

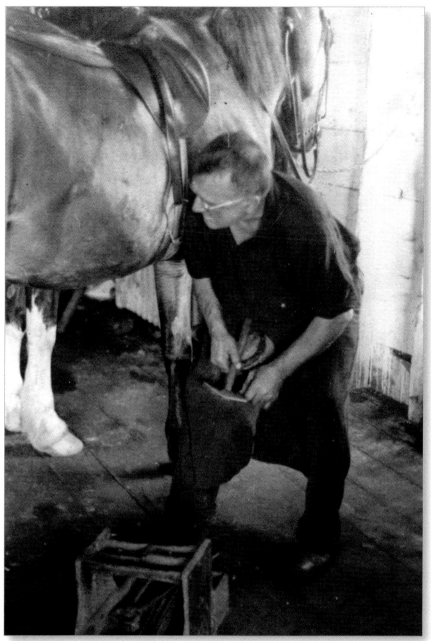

Blacksmith Orrin Norton shoes the horse Laddie at his shop on Dock Street in Edgartown.

exploring, or swimming. And one of my greatest pleasures in the early forties was driving a tractor to mow the meadow next to Poucha Pond. It was not work, but a pleasure for me.

Emma Mayhew Whiting, grandmother of the famous Island painter Allen Whiting, wrote a poem when she, too, was working her land in West Tisbury many years ago. It evokes the sense of peace and satisfaction that a farmer has for his labors. Her granddaughter Tara, who is a captain on the Chappy ferry in the summer, gave me permission to reprint it here. It speaks for itself.

> *Oh, who am I, Lord, who am I*
> *That I should have the sea and sky,*
> *That I should own this bit of land;*
> *Be fore ordained to understand*
> *The lowly language of the earth,*
> *In primal tasks to find life's worth.*
> *Ah, bursting is my thankful heart*
> *My fate is not the crowded mart*
> *For thou in kindness destined me*
> *To love my meadow by the sea.*

*The bell attached to the flagpole called the
Welch family to dinner each night.*

Chapter Four

THE FARM HOUSE

THE FARM HOUSE WAS VERY DIFFERENT IN 1933 FROM the house that exists today. A much smaller structure, it consisted of just a medium-sized room with two very small rooms adjacent to it. The upstairs was identical, like a box on top of a box. The ceilings were so low on the second floor that an adult couldn't stand up straight. The windows were small, hard to open, and held open with a notched stick. The north side of the house had no windows at all, to protect the house from the cold north winds.

The only insulation was seaweed and corncobs. The seaweed is still visible on the first floor behind some very old, extra-wide wall boards. The corncobs appeared when the bedroom walls were torn out on the second floor.

Narrow stairs, measuring twenty-two inches wide, went up steeply along the north wall. The stairs were so narrow, steep, and hazardous, we were not allowed to carry lighted lamps or candles to the second floor.

The Farm House, photographed in 1929, had no electricity or running water. While it has been remodeled, all of it is intact today.

When my father bought the farm, two additions had been added to the house. One was a kitchen to the north of the original house, and the other was a small room to the south (now the bedroom I share with my husband, Bob). Because of the difficulty of getting to Edgartown for church, the Vieras had their own small prayer space, and this room was their chapel.

The kitchen was where the front hall is now. A good-sized room, that original kitchen was the heart of the home. A big, black, cast-iron stove was the centerpiece of the kitchen. Patented in the late 1800s, it has probably been used in the house for about a century. Originally a wood-burning stove, it was switched to coal when we first came to Chappy and finally converted to two kerosene burners that are still used today. It served as a heat source as well as for cooking. It also dried the laundry that was washed in a tub by a local woman. Wet clothes hung over the stove on a rack, and boots were lined up in front of it to dry.

Once you got used to using the stove, it was the best stove in the world, even though you had to turn a cake around in the oven halfway through its cooking time because the heat came from only one side. It wasn't as hot as a gas stove, but its flexibility was, and is, perfect: places on it to boil, simmer, raise bread, and warm plates.

A white painted dining table with a white metal top seated six people and was indestructible. A chrome-plated hand pump was our only water supply at one end of a sink behind the stove in an alcove we called the pantry. The alcove held jars from summer canning.

A large shiny kettle on the stove steamed quietly, ready for tea, for washing dishes, and for warming cold bathwater. The stove always seemed to have numerous pots and black cast-iron fry pans from which came tantalizing aromas. At the evening meal, a kerosene lamp stood in the middle of the metal-topped table, plates were warming on the shelf of the stove, and a pitcher of fresh raw milk sat on the sideboard. We filled our plates with food almost entirely from the farm and sat at the table with our parents.

MY MOTHER WAS NOT A GOOD COOK, EVEN THOUGH HER mother had sent her to Fanny Farmer Cooking School in Boston before she was married. Fortunately, my father loved to cook and enjoyed experimenting and serving unusual foods. From his fishing boat, *Walrus,* he once caught a huge sea turtle, part of which he cooked for dinner. It tasted like chicken. We frequently ate shark. It tasted like swordfish. We often ate eels that were delicious. You ate the meat off the segments of their backbone with your fingers. It tasted like chicken. One experiment he didn't repeat was his effort to cook skunk. I think we all rebelled because of the smell. He even tried crow, but that, too, was not a success.

My father added excitement by bringing a live goat or pony into the kitchen on occasion. We three girls thought it was hilarious, and my mother was tolerant with his hijinks. When an addition was built onto the house in 1934, we had a real dining room and no longer ate in the kitchen. That

Ruth Welch, Edo's mother, standing outside the Farm House's front porch.

didn't slow down my father. He still brought the pony in to walk around the table. He put an Audubon print on the wall directly in front of my mother's seat, showing a hawk tearing apart and eating a duck. It is still there today, though the room is no longer a dining room.

On our first visit to the farm in the winter of 1932, we depended on kerosene lamps as there was no electricity. The only heat besides the black kitchen stove was the square brown parlor stove, also kerosene. It heated the rest of the house. In the ceiling of the sitting room two registers allowed warm air to circulate upstairs, although those bedrooms were never really warm.

I slept in one of the small bedrooms downstairs, on a thin horsehair mattress, piled high with blankets. Getting out of the warm bed was a challenge. I still remember the sound of the coal being shaken down in the grate of the black stove and would try to time getting up and dressed so I could scoot into the kitchen and warm up with my back to that warm black monster. With no running water and therefore no bathroom, we had a choice of using a chamber pot and then dumping and cleaning it later, or making a run for the outhouse that used to be close to the Farm House.

In the middle 1930s my father got a generator, called a Kohler. It sat firmly on a cement floor in a shed behind the barn. That gave us running water, a bathroom of sorts upstairs, and a new sink in the kitchen. It also provided a few lights and ran a small refrigerator. The bathroom was over the kitchen, with a vent in the floor directly over the stove. The delicious warmth from the stove made the bathroom the warmest room in the house. The vent also allowed sounds to carry upstairs and we delighted in eavesdropping on the adult conversations. To get to the bathroom we bent over almost double to go through a small door and an attic, both about four and a half feet high, but it was far better than running outdoors.

MY MOTHER'S GREATEST JOY WAS THE REFRIGERATOR. IT was small and didn't keep things very cold, but at least she didn't have to go outside to a gray wooden chest on legs, called an icebox, that resided in "the outside pantry." My mother would chip small pieces of ice with an ice pick from a big chunk to cool our beverages. An ice pond behind a

The finished farm house, circa 1934, after boatbuilder Manuel Swartz finished renovations.

neighbor's house was in a deep kettle hole, made by the glacier. In the winter the men on Chappy would gather to cut the ice into large chunks and haul them to the icehouse at the edge of the pond. The ice cakes would be carefully laid out on straw on the floor of the icehouse and covered with another layer of straw. Each new layer of ice would be covered and built up until the icehouse was full. The only alternative to the ice that was delivered by year-round resident Moses Jeffers was to go to the ferry and pick up ice there – but you had a much smaller chunk by the time it got to the farm.

In 1933 my father hired Manuel Swartz to build an addition to the Farm House. Swartz, who had his shop in what's now the Old Sculpin Gallery (Old Sculpin was his nickname), was a boatbuilder by trade, but during the Depression he had no boats to build, so he happily took on the challenge of our addition.

The new addition started just behind the stove wall in the sitting room and included new stairs to the second floor and a new basement. A hallway to a front door made it more modern. The new living room with its large fireplace was spacious to us. A big sofa faced the fireplace, and behind it, near a window, was my father's desk and eventually a telephone.

During one particularly bad thunderstorm, a round ball of lightning came through the window, ruined the phone, went across the floor, up and over the sofa between my mother and a friend sitting there, and across the floor and up the chimney. After that we were never allowed to talk on the phone in a thunderstorm.

Farm Houses
ALL THE PLACES WE LIVE

The farm includes five houses other than the main house, each with its own story.

The **Webquish House** was owned by Lydia Webquish, a Wampanoag, who had inherited the house and twenty-three acres adja-

cent to our property from her father. Although she never married, a minister lived in the cellar that had a dirt floor and a window. A small organ occupied a special spot in the small living room, and I can picture the minister coming up from

Webquish House

the cellar through the trap door that connected through the bedroom closet, and conducting church services accompanied by organ music.

Rumor has it that the ghost of the minister still haunts the house. After World War II, my mother rented Webquish House to tenants who claimed they heard the minister's ghost. The tenants would put something heavy over the trapdoor leading to the cellar where he lived, to be sure the ghost stayed below.

Today Webquish belongs to my sister, Ruth. The original part of the house is one of the three oldest on Chappy.

The **Gomes' House** had an early history that included betrayal and intrigue. Annie Gomes, a Wampanoag, had been a neighbor as long as I can remember. She had lived for years with her friend, Oscar, and had written a deed to Oscar for the house. When they had a falling out, Oscar moved into a shack that belonged to another Chappy resident and gave him the deed to the house in lieu of rent. Sometime after that, the owner of the shack persuaded Annie to go off-island to a nursing home, thereby acquiring the house.

My family was concerned as to what would happen to the Gomes House, which sits on a knoll just inside the gate to the farm and was close to our driveway. After some tense negotiations, we were able to buy it. The house then became my sister, Hope's, summer home.

And, finally, there are **Drake's Nest** and the **Gunning Camp**, both acquired in the original purchase of the land in 1928 and the only houses on the farm that haven't had a major addition or renovation.

Drake's Nest was given its name because Frank Drake and his

Drake's Nest in 1920, before a small addition.

family moved in when my father shifted from hunting to farming. The house is tiny, yet a family with eight children lived there; when a new baby was born, one of the older children moved out.

The front part is the original building, and it looks like an Oak Bluffs campground cottage. It is narrow and tall with just enough room under the roof to include two small bedrooms upstairs. Under the steep eaves there is barely enough headroom for a short adult or a child to stand. Two cots can be squeezed into each room.

For many years, our cousins, the Tylers, lived there year round, but now it has become a place where some of the fourth generation stay when they come to work in the summer. Despite the outhouse and outside shower, they are happy to be there and usually have numerous friends and guests to keep things lively on the farm. It's a busy scene.

The Gunning Camp, which was really all my father was interested in when he bought the first one hundred acres, was dragged over the ice during a very cold winter when my father had no more use for it on Poucha Pond. It was moved on skids over the frozen marsh by a pair of workhorses to its present site at the head of the meadow with a distant view of Poucha Pond and East Beach. The tower where the hunters sat to spot the geese coming in to the decoys was removed. A wide porch was added, but otherwise, it looks as it did in 1932.

The screened porch was the best part of the Camp. One end held a table with benches for eating or writing. A double bed at the other end was like sleeping outdoors. You can see the moon and stars and hear the crickets, the owls, and wonderful night sounds. In the middle was a sitting area. Now that the Camp is used year-round, the porch has Plexiglas windows that can be installed in inclement weather.

(Left) The Camp, with its tower removed, was moved from the narrows at Poucha Pond to a new home closer to the Farm House (below).

Kevin Keady, who first came to us as a summer worker, has become a permanent resident of the Camp. Kevin has renovated the Camp, adding landscaping and window boxes. He insulated and redid the kitchen and turned part of the bunkroom into an office where he composes lyrics in the winter and creates music. Painting, shingling, and general repairs keep him busy.

The only modern house on the farm is the **Garden House**. We built the house for Nelson Jones, who came to the farm in 1987. He had worked at the last dairy in Edgartown until its close and came to us at the suggestion of the dairy owner, our son Stephen. Nelson has been our Rock of Gibraltar for more than twenty years, fixing equipment, doing woodwork, growing vegetables, haying, tending animals, and doing anything that is needed on a working farm.

Charlie Welch with year-round resident Sally Jeffers look out over the island.

Chapter Five

OUR MOSTLY EMPTY ISLAND

WE WERE ON CHAPPAQUIDDICK FROM THE DAY SCHOOL let out at the end of May until the day before school started at the end of September. The anticipation of that time was as exciting to us as Christmas. There were not enough hours in the day or days in the week to do all we wanted to do, and we dreamed up all sorts of adventures.

An endless stretch of glorious days was filled with all those exciting but nebulous things that children can find to do on a mostly empty island. No one worried about us getting lost, since we were on an island so open and treeless that in places you could see from one shore to the other. We came so early that there were no summer folk and stayed later than most in September. Even in July and August only a few families with children our ages summered here, since there were only about fifteen summer houses on Chappy in the early 1930s and even fewer year-round residents.

The first summer we spent there, my parents brought a nursemaid to take care of us. She didn't like the isolation and didn't return, leaving us to run free. Although my parents tried once or twice more to bring nursemaids, they eventually gave up. So there we were, three very different sisters eager for fun. Ruth was the oldest, the ringleader, the creative and imaginative sister. She was taller, stronger, and cleverer. I was in the middle, always ready for new adventures no matter what they were. Hope, two years younger, was full of fun and mischief and had an infectious giggle.

We had to entertain ourselves. There was no Edgartown Yacht Club membership, no Beach Club, and no way to get to Edgartown, except on foot across the land bridge that was wiped away in 2007 by a winter storm or on foot three miles to the Chappy ferry. Yet we had access to beaches all over the island, played in streams, visited neighbors, and had endless fun in the woods, fields, and ponds. We loved to dam up the muddy, freshwater springs in the marsh or the saltwater creeks that flowed into Cape Pogue Pond. By the end of the day, we were wet, salty, or muddy.

Our days always included some hours of hard farmwork, which was expected of us, but there was plenty of time for the pleasures of growing up on this beautiful island. The beaches were empty and clean and filled with gifts from the sea like glass buoys from Portugal and lobster pot buoys from Maine. We proudly brought them all home to our parents.

Every so often we would come across pieces of the wreck of the *Mertie B. Crowley*, driven into Wasque Point by a storm in 1910. Over the years the wreck was buried in the sand, but

Horses gave children an unusual freedom. Here, from left, Ann Child, Bess Anthony, Ruth and Hope Welch at the Point across from Edgartown.

parts of her would suddenly appear anywhere between the Cape Pogue Lighthouse and Wasque after a bad storm.

Since my father believed children should neither be seen nor heard, we were sent outdoors in the morning and not allowed back in until lunch and then out again until dinner time. He was firm in this rule; since we often came to the kitchen door asking for a drink of water, my father installed an outside drinking fountain we called a "bubbler." When we wanted to come in to use the new and only bathroom, we were reminded that there was an outhouse close by.

Farm horses my father brought to the island gave us mobility and freedom. We would set off in the morning with lunches, bathing suits, and extra clothes in our saddlebags or tied around our waist, and be gone all day. On rainy days we holed up in our own secret places to play or read or think.

RUTH DECIDED ONE SUMMER WE NEEDED A CLUBHOUSE, our own space. We discovered an old abandoned building where my father had formerly raised turkeys to sell to the summer people. It was dark and smelly with no windows and only a small front door for light and air. No adult could stand up inside, so we knew we were safe from prying eyes.

Ruth and Edo at the Lion's Hotel, with their faithful dog Trixie.

We found odd bits of flotsam around the farm to serve as seats and a table. With books and a hand-cranked Victrola, it was our refuge on rainy days.

The lingering smell of turkeys got into our clothes and hair. Whether it was the smell we brought into the Farm House, or whether our parents felt sorry for us I don't know, but they eventually bought us a wonderful dark green painted building called a Hodgson House. It was a prefabricated kit with two rooms separated by a door and a screen that went from the rafters to the ceiling to give ventilation between the rooms.

Our little house was small and simple, with each room measuring only twelve feet square and a front porch that was twelve feet by four feet. The back room was used as a guest room and was off limits. The front room was our castle. The linoleum floor, brightly colored and indestructible, was a game board, with a large checkerboard and other games set into it.

A rolltop desk (a real one, albeit child-sized), a table, small chairs, and stove provided us with all we needed. We weren't allowed to use the stove, but it looked important. Yellow curtains adorned the two windows inside; the front porch, shady and cool since the house was set into the pine woods, gave us respite on hot days. We spent every rainy day there, reading, writing, and playing games.

We called our Hodgson House the Lion's Hotel. The name came from a set of red and white plates in the Farm House that showed a coach and four horses in front of an English pub, the Red Lion Inn. The turkey house had been

Farm horse Big Bill, who was aptly named for his size and strength.

named just that, and we even painted a sign for it. But our new quarters were such an improvement we felt it deserved a grander name.

WE EXPLORED THE ISLAND CONSTANTLY, ALWAYS FINDING things that were new and exciting. Sometimes we would discover just-hatched baby ducklings frantically swimming in line behind their mother who was regally leading them to safety; or a family of otters, humping along like seals or sliding down a slope joyously.

Poucha Pond was one of our favorite places. A freshwater pond until the 1950s, it was a treasure trove of wildlife. A solid dike, connecting the main part of Chappy to East Beach, blocked the flow of water between the lagoon to the north and Poucha Pond to the south. A flume in the dike on

Big Bill
THE WORKHORSE

My father found a huge, gentle, suitable horse at a stable in Falmouth, not too far from Woods Hole. He wanted to bring it to the farm to pull the farm equipment and for other farm chores.

Since this was long before the days of truck-pulled horse trailers, my father's solution for the first section of the trip was to get someone to walk the horse from the stable to Woods Hole. My father and I met the horse, Big Bill, in Wood's Hole, walked him onto the ferry Nobska, and tied him to a stanchion on the car deck. (During those days, you often saw horses and cows tied up among the cars on the Nobska or the old Martha's Vineyard.)

When we got to Oak Bluffs, we walked Big Bill to the road at the top of the hill toward Edgartown. My father handed me the rope and said, "I'll meet you at the Chappy ferry. Just don't let Big Bill step on you." He disappeared in his car over the next rise, and there I was, alone, with Bill's rope in my hand.

Big Bill and I hesitantly started off. He seemed willing to follow me, and I kept my distance from those big feet. We went down Beach Road to Edgartown, a narrow, unimproved road with no bicycle path. Big Bill seemed careful about where he put his feet, and passersby seemed impressed to see a freckled, skinny redhead, about nine years old, leading an enormous horse down an empty road.

We made it safely into Edgartown and down Main Street to the Chappy ferry. I don't remember how we got him across the ferry and the rest of the way home, but Big Bill seemed to consider me a friend from then on.

the beach end allowed fresh water to build up in the pond during the fall and winter. A gate hinged at the top allowed excess water to push it open and spill out from the pond into the lagoon on the north side of the dike but prevented saltwater from coming in.

In the spring the gate was opened, and the built-up head of fresh water rushed out. Herring (technically known as alewives) swam in against the strong flow to spawn in the fresh water. The water level in the pond was allowed to drop until the marshes became dry in the summer, dry enough to cut hay. Then the flume was closed to prevent saltwater coming in.

The marsh hay made wonderful bedding for the farm animals and excellent mulch for the garden, as it had no weed seeds in it. Until recently the rusty remains of a horse-drawn mower could be seen, abandoned at the edge of what is now a wetlands. Horses were used to cut salt hay instead of a tractor because a tractor would have sunk into the marsh irretrievably.

The herring run was controlled by the Pease family, who owned Tom's Neck Farm as well as both sides of the Lagoon. Shipping boxes full of herring to Boston, New York, and beyond was a good business. Some of the herring scales

Looking toward Dike Road from the Farm House. The bantam hen house is to the right, with Tom's Neck Farm in the distance.

The pony Babe safely housed for the day.

were made into "pearls" by a business in Katama in Edgar-town and called "Priscilla Pearls." The pond was controlled by an organization of riparian owners called the Poucha Pond Fish and Meadow Company.

The herring were stored in oblong cars in the water until it was time to ship them off-island in wooden barrels. The Pease family built three wooden buildings on the edge of the pond at the far side of the dike. I remember empty wooden barrels in two of the buildings and the tools they needed to catch the herring. A smaller building with bunks was used for a hunting camp. Since no one locked doors, we used to poke around in the dark and smelly buildings, thinking they were very exciting places.

When I was young, the pond was a freshwater water-fowl habitat, filled with blue crabs and perch. The most fun for me on Poucha Pond was the perch fishing. Yellow perch were plentiful, and with a leaky rowboat stashed at the end of the meadow and a line with a sinker and some bait, we would spend happy hours sitting in the middle of the pond, in the sun, on the sparkling water, pulling up perch every few minutes until we had a small bucket full. I never became an avid saltwater fisherman, probably because I was spoiled by the ease of catching fish on Poucha Pond.

At times the ducks and geese darkened the sky and shadowed the pond because of their large numbers. The fresh water was full of duck weed and wild celery, among other good food that waterfowl loved. The number of birds was awesome. When the wind was southeast, you could hear the ducks and geese gabbling like a group of ladies having tea. On a still evening you could hear them all the way to the Farm House.

Ralph Harding, our year-round neighbor who worked for the family for sixty-three years, trapped muskrats in the marshes and the pond, sending the skins to New York City to be sold and made into fur coats. Eventually, muskrats became too scarce to trap. Otters, too, became scarce, although they and the muskrats have made a comeback. In a cold winter when the ponds are frozen and a coating of snow is on the ground, these playful "critters" slide down a bank on the snow, out onto the ice, then climb back up the hill to do it all over again.

Later, after a lot of controversy, the Town of Edgartown took the dike from the Pease family by eminent domain, believing there would be better scalloping in Cape Pogue Pond and in Poucha Pond if Poucha were salt instead of fresh water. In 1952 the dike was breached to the Lagoon by the town. The water at the south end, near Wasque, is now brackish and too warm for scallops.

ALTHOUGH WE LOVED RIDING BAREBACK ON THE WORK-horses, we were thrilled to be given a small black Shetland pony named Cozy. Cozy came to us when the youngest of four neighboring siblings outgrew her. She pulled a small cart, just big enough for two small children, and we went everywhere on Chappy in it; to picnics, birthday parties, vis-iting, and to the beach. Cozy loved to swim, and if we hung onto her tail, she would pull us along in the water. It was glorious fun.

When Cozy was thirty-six years old (very long years even for a pony), my sister Hope and I went to a birthday party on North Neck. Of course, we showed off our won-derful pony and how she loved to swim. Afterward we left Cozy tied to a post while we enjoyed the party. Hitching her up to her cart after the party, we drove her home and stopped in front of the barn, and, while still sitting in the cart, told our father about the party. Cozy waited patiently. When Hope and I stepped out of the cart, Cozy lay down and never got up. She died shortly thereafter.

My father tried to console me by saying she was an old pony and her day had come, but I knew I had caused her

Hope and Edo sit on the running board of the delivery truck.

demise by letting her stand in a cold wind when she was wet. It was one of the most devastating things in my life, and it took me years to get over it.

SUMMER'S END WAS NEVER WELCOMED BY US, YET OUR occasional trips in the winter were awesome experiences.

Sometimes during a very cold January, Cape Pogue Pond would freeze over completely. One year, in the thirties, it froze so hard that Gerry Jeffers, a year-round resident who now owns the Chappy Store, drove a car across the ice from his family's house on the pond to the lighthouse on the

A winter visit in the 1930s gave a different look to Chappaquiddick.

opposite side. He used to fix up old cars for his friends, and they would race each other on the ice, trying to see who was the best at making his vehicle skid in circles.

Our boathouse on the shoreline since 1932 has withstood almost all the gales and hurricanes. In warm weather we used it to store our boats and as a place to hold family clambakes and change into our bathing suits.

But in the winter, everything changed. One winter, when the ice was particularly thick, a winter gale from the northeast broke up the solid ice into huge chunks, some the size of a small car, and sent them hurtling up onto the beach and eight feet into the boathouse, destroying the doors and damaging the boats stored inside.

When we were young the water's edge was well out beyond the large rocks to the left of the boathouse. A pier in front of the boathouse jutted out into the water. It was a great place to sit and play, but it disappeared in another storm when huge ice chunks destroyed it. Now it is very shoal, and a pier would be useless. The old spiles from the pier built in 1932 are still visible at low tide despite the shoaling and increased water level.

It is a reminder that our island may, someday, return to the sea.

Frank Drake, skating at "Black Joe's Pond"
off the road to Meeting House Hill.

Chapter Six

OUR COMMUNITY

C HAPPAQUIDDICK WAS A UNIQUE COMMUNITY IN THE 1930s and early 1940s, partly because there were so few people on the island and partly because it was a very close community. There was a feeling of belonging, of warmth and friendliness, of helping one another when there was a need.

It was a do-it-yourself community or an "ask your neighbor for help" community, since it was difficult to find repair people willing to come to Chappy. Each neighbor had a skill that could be called upon in an emergency, and they were always ready to help.

While emergencies might come in different forms, community support was most apparent when there was a fire. Since there was no electricity on Chappy until the late 1930s, we lived with kerosene lamps, candles, fireplaces, and stoves. There was no fire engine and only a small number of dedicated volunteers living on the island. We were all acutely conscious of the dangers of fire.

Each family had its own set of firefighting tools. Large sturdy brooms – until recently kept in the rafters of our garage as symbols of the old days – were used to beat out brush fires, which we did as if our lives depended on it. We used shovels to dig trenches as fire breaks to try to stop a fire, and grabbed buckets to form bucket brigades that might be fifteen people long.

Sometimes Edgartown firemen would try to come to our aid. Long before a fire truck was stationed on Chappaquiddick, the fire department in Edgartown tried to bring a small fire truck over to Chappy on the first motorized ferry, the *City of Chappaquiddick*, for a fire at Wasque Farm. Hurrying to get there, the driver of the truck gunned the motor and skidded the tires off the planks on the Chappy side, causing the truck to fall into the water. Not totally immersed, the front end jutted up in the air on dry land but the rear was in the water. There it stayed until someone could figure out how to extricate it. In the meantime, Leo Gill's chicken house at Wasque Farm burned to the ground. The foundation is still visible.

Most fires were fought by hand. Word spread quickly and every able-bodied man, woman, and child showed up. Year-round resident Casmede Bettencourt's house, beyond our farm's Drake's Nest, caught fire because a full bottle of water had been left on a wooden table in the sun. The magnification of the sun's rays through the bottle of water caused the table to ignite. The only available water to fight

A lighthouse keeper's truck slips off the ferry when the brakes failed to hold.

the fire was a hand pump near the road that goes by Drake's Nest, about 200 yards distance. All sorts of people appeared with their buckets. Two people took turns manning the hand pump, and the rest of us lined up and passed the full buckets from hand to hand until the bucket reached the house. The last one in line ran the empty buckets back to the pump.

Although I was only ten years old, I remember vividly the tremendous fatigue and sense of urgency to keep those buckets moving, and the sense of relief and pride when it was all over. The small kitchen wing where the fire started was burned badly, but the rest of the house was saved.

The Chappy volunteer firemen have always been a remarkable bunch, whose wry motto is, "We never lost a foundation." They even had the first female firefighter in Edgartown, Marion Harding, who lived near the fire station when it was built. She was often the first person to arrive at the station when it housed a small fire engine. She learned how to drive the truck, and one night she arrived in her pajamas and wrapper and got the truck to the fire before anyone else.

A HIGHLIGHT OF OUR SUMMER WAS A CLAMBAKE PUT ON BY my father and a group of his friends. People like Manuel Swartz, Dr. James Wilson, Sheriff Tom Dexter, and several other Edgartown friends were always available, experienced and ready to help, and it took all of them and more to pull

Frank Drake heats the stones for a summer clambake.

Sally Jeffers
AN ISLAND MATRIARCH

*S*ally Jeffers was a matriarch. She had come to Chappy from the Deep South as a cook for a summer family many years before I knew her in the 1930s. She married Moses Jeffers, who lived and farmed off Jeffers Lane. After Moses died, Sally (or Mrs. Jeffers, as we called her) stayed on with her two step-daughters, Gladys and Tillie.

Mrs. Jeffers ran a restaurant in the house overlooking Cape Pogue Pond called "The Chappaquiddick Outlook." She was a good southern cook, and her pies were the best in the world, filled to overflowing with freshly picked wild blueberries gathered by Gladys and Tillie.

Her restaurant was a formal one. She always wore a black hat, and Gladys and Tillie had white starched aprons. When we went to the restaurant, we had to be squeaky clean and dressed in our best clothes. The men always wore a coat and tie. My mother and father enjoyed taking guests there, especially friends from West Chop and Boston, who always thought Chappy was uncivilized and nothing but sand dunes.

After Mrs. Jeffers died, Gladys and Tillie continued to live in the house near the road and carried on the restaurant overlooking Cape Pogue Pond until they were too old to continue. They also prepared meals for summer people, when asked, making dinners for housebound people and delivering them to their door. This was Chappy's version of "takeout."

Watermelon was the ultimate treat at the end of a clambake.

off a clambake. The bakes were held at the beach at Cape Pogue Pond, and the boathouse was utilized to store the preparations, to serve the food, and as shelter in case of rain.

The preparations started weeks ahead of time.

First we gathered rocks to heat the bake. Someone drove the farm truck along the edge of fields where farmers had thrown rocks over many years when clearing their land. The rocks had to be a certain size, not too big and not too small, and every clambake required a new batch because they either cracked or lost their ability to get really hot once they were used.

Then we had to find seaweed to go on top of the heated rocks, to create the steam that cooked the bake. The seaweed had to be rockweed, the brown seaweed that attaches itself to rocks and has bubbles on the stems that are like miniature balloons, fun to pop with your fingers. Rockweed is not prevalent on Chappy because there are so few rocks at water's edge. When we found some, we collected it in burlap grain bags from the farm and left the bags at water's edge to keep the seaweed wet until it was needed the day of the bake.

The day of the bake started at dawn. All the food had to be gathered and tied up in homemade cheesecloth bags and carefully laid out on long tables in the boathouse. The pit to heat the rocks had been dug on the beach several days before and filled with oak firewood with the rocks among them. The fire was started early by pouring kerosene on the wood and burned vigorously for a long time with flames reaching toward the sky. It was a spectacular sight, almost as good as the Fourth of July.

Frank Drake was the master planner on the clambakes and made the decisions. At Frank's word the fire was pulled apart, and the remains of the wood were thrown into the water with a loud hiss. The rocks were taken out one by one with shovels and put in the shallow pit or depression made in the sand. Care had to be taken to keep out any of the charred wood, since it would spoil the taste of the food.

Next came the bags of rockweed. Even the adults would gather around and marvel at the heat of the rocks, the smell of the rockweed, and the sizzling noise it made when it was dumped on the hot rocks in the pit.

Then came the food, each layer carefully wrapped in cheesecloth. Bags of potatoes, sausages, onions, chicken, corn, clams, and finally the lobsters were carefully placed on the hissing and steaming rockweed. More rockweed was spread on top of the food, and a huge tarp was thrown over the whole pile. The edges of the tarp, which was an old canvas sail no longer fit for sailing, were weighted down by shovelfuls of sand. Frank then inspected the mound to be sure that no steam was escaping to cool off the bake.

While the food cooked, the adults enjoyed their "libations," either standing around the mound or sitting on the benches by the long tables. The children's job was to set the tables and to line up the big plates at one end and smaller plates for the watermelon at the other.

When the bake was deemed done by Frank, everyone gathered while two or three people pulled off the sail. The smell is indescribable. Steam poured out through the seaweed and wafted around. Finally the seaweed came off with pitchforks and revealed the cheesecloth bags of food underneath, slightly colored a brownish red by the seaweed.

With broomsticks and similar tools, each bag was carefully picked up and gingerly carried to the end of the long tables in the boathouse.

As the wonderful smells filled the boathouse, people brought their plates and were served by Frank. After that, it was all eating and enthusiastic compliments.

ALTHOUGH THE CLAMBAKE WAS THE SUMMER'S BEST EATING, community cooperation was equally essential when my family needed to slaughter an animal to provide us with food for the winter.

Casmede Bettencourt was called upon for the slaughtering and butchering. Casmede was the father of ferry operator Tony Bettencourt and grandfather of Foster Silva, both Chappaquiddick legends. Casmede worked for my father when the farm was first starting up. He was short and strong and was wonderful at cutting wood for the stoves in the winter.

Each year Casmede, who was our nearest neighbor, slaughtered a pig that had grown up on the farm. The pig was hauled up by its hind feet through a hole in the ceiling of the barn. At just the right height Casmede dispatched the pig quickly with a knife to its throat, and then gathered the blood in a clean pail to make "blood pudding," a dish the Portuguese brought to the island and important to Portuguese celebrations.

Casmede Bettencourt and Frank Drake shown in 1938 cutting firewood.

Casmede's wife took the intestines to her kitchen and made sausages out of them, filling them with ground pork. She had a tub of water with oranges and lemons in it, and she washed the intestines over and over again, pushing them inside out with a long straight stick and finally stuffing them with the sausage meat.

Mrs. Bettencourt also made head cheese from small bits of meat parts picked from the head of the pig and cooked until they formed a jellylike substance. Put into a crock in the cellar, the head cheese lasted indefinitely. Brought up from the cellar as a special treat and served on crackers as hors d'oeuvres, it was considered delicious.

It seemed that all the able-bodied men on the island gathered for the pig slaughter. Always willing to help, they were repaid with a share of the pig. It was a gathering or a "happening," and a good time was had by all, except for the pig and me.

EVEN IN THE WINTER THE SENSE OF COMMUNITY WAS strong. Charlie Welch's Gunning Stand on Poucha Pond was a gathering place for an eclectic group of men from 1929 to 1933.

Men came from all over the Vineyard and the mainland to join a "shoot" at my father's stand. Off-island gunners considered it a special place, and my father welcomed all comers.

The Gunning Camp sat on a hillock or "island" in the marsh at the narrowest part of Poucha Pond. The one-story

The island's dogs got a good scrubbing, with proceeds going to the Edgartown MSPCA.

gray building with a lookout tower contained a bunk room with two sets of bunk beds and a main room with a large black woodstove that provided heat, food, and hot water. A large shiny teakettle always simmering in the winter gave the room a cozy feeling. One wall of the main room had a sink with a hand pump and shelves for pots and pans and china. A round table for eating, drinking, and playing cards stood in front of the stove. An alcove provided space for an additional bed. The space was small but cozy and comfortable, especially on stormy days.

The blinds, where the hunters crouched so as not to scare the wild birds, were built at the Narrows on Poucha Pond by the former owner, but my father refurbished them and built longer blinds along the waterfront. The blinds consisted of two fences with a walkway between. The posts from the old blinds can still be seen along the edge of the marsh, but everything else has been removed or washed away.

The last island on the point at the narrows of Poucha Pond, where the camp was built in 1928, was much larger and more heavily vegetated than it is now. One of the first things my father did was to build a "causeway" over the first marsh to the first island. Ralph Harding hauled gravel from the beach at Cape Pogue Pond in the back of a small pickup truck, loading, unloading, and spreading it by hand with the

A day at the beach, with a refreshing dip and some excellent gifts from the sea.

heavy square-ended coal shovel that is still in the barn. The twelve-inch pipe that Ralph installed to drain the upper marshes is still there, but the sea level has increased so much in eighty years that the water washes over the dike as well as through the pipe.

When the federal government banned live decoys, my father gave up gunning on the Poucha marshes. Since he still enjoyed shooting and the camaraderie he had known at the camp, he took up trap shooting, then skeet shooting, both using clay pigeons.

Skeet shooting is quite different from trap. Trap has one low house from which a clay pigeon is thrown either by hand or mechanically. With skeet, there are three buildings from which the clay pigeons are thrown, today by mechanical means, which makes them go farther and more unpredictably than with trap. In the 1930s the throwing was done by a person who could change the angle to make it a more challenging target. One person stood in a shelter behind the row of shooting stations and pulled on an upright pole connected to the low house to automatically send a clay pigeon flying. The sport takes speed and great skill.

Skeet shooting became an island-wide favorite, as popular on the Vineyard in the 1920s and 1930s as surf fishing is today. My father's hunting friends were his skeet-shooting buddies. The skeet range was known as Sidelinger's Gun Club, named for Ernest Q. Sidelinger, who lived in what is now called Wasque Farm. After damaging his hand working on a fishing boat, Sidelinger came ashore on Chappy and never left. He was a character who loved nothing better than to wrap himself in a huge muskrat coat and peek in windows to scare people like my mother, which he did very successfully. The first time she saw the apparition at the living room window she thought it was a bear.

In return for his pranks, the men retaliated by teasing Sidelinger unmercifully, and it was an ongoing competition to see who could create the best practical joke; once they towed Sidelinger around in a bathtub behind a truck. Sidelinger never missed a shoot, either because he was a crack shot or just because he enjoyed the conviviality.

Charlie Welch and his friend, Ernest Q. Sidelinger, wearing his muskrat coat.

Several years ago, two men from Minnesota came to Chappy with Tom Taylor, an ardent target shooter and hunter in Edgartown, to see what they described as the "oldest skeet range in the country." Pimpneymouse Farm's range is considered the oldest because the first skeet range in Andover, Massachusetts, was discontinued many years earlier and moved to a larger location. The second skeet range in the country, ours, has continued to operate on Pimpneymouse Farm, off and on.

We learned that the original skeet range lost out to house lots, as have most ranges built in the 1920s and 1930s, growth having overtaken them. We also learned that the mechanisms that threw the clay pigeons are valuable antiques,

Babe and Lucille at the ferry house, waiting patiently for riders to return from Edgartown.

and our visitors hoped we would one day donate them to a skeet-shooting museum.

It was traditional to have a competition or "shoot" during the weekend of February 22, Washington's Birthday, at Linger's Gun Club. Men from the mainland as well as all the towns on the island enjoyed the competition, fun, and camaraderie.

In 1932 the gunners from the four towns banded together and presented my father with a magnificent pewter punch bowl at the February shoot, with thanks for the good times they had on Pimpneymouse Farm.

Tom Dexter, who was the sheriff on the Vineyard when I was a child and a regular at the Gunning Stand, wrote a poem about a bet he made with my father. It is framed with the dollar bill he paid to my father and hangs on a wall in the Farm House. It gives an idea of the fun that went on at the camp.

> *This is the bill Tom Dexter paid,*
> *To settle up the bet he made*
> *On Swartz and Welch's marksmanship*
> *While on a Poucha gunning trip,*
> *And 'tis preserved herewith today*
> *That gunners of the future may*
> *Be taught that by descriptive plan*
> *The sheriff failed to get his man.*

The sidewheel steamer Nantucket, *coming from Woods Hole to Oak Bluffs.*

Chapter Seven

OUR SUMMER PEOPLE

THERE WERE ONLY ABOUT THIRTY SUMMER HOUSES IN the early 1930s when we first started spending long summer months on Pimpneymouse Farm, and not that many more in the 1940s. Five were on North Neck, eleven from Wasque along Katama Bay to the "Point" (now the ferry landing), several near the Beach Club, and the rest on Menaca Hill across from the Beach Club. The Katama people didn't know the North Neck people, and the Menaca Hill people didn't know anyone unless they were related to them.

Living in the middle of the island and having horses, we knew everyone in this small community. The land was so open we could gallop full tilt across grassy fields to the top of Meeting House Hill, and as children on ponies, we were welcomed everywhere we went.

The summer people came for three months, bringing their trunks and their livestock, including their cows, to assure a supply of fresh milk. Although they left their wagons stored on Chappy all year, they brought horses each summer to pull the wagons. Because all the summer houses were on the water, the easiest form of transportation to Edgartown, Cape Pogue Pond, and South Beach was by sailboat, and many of the summer people had catboats built by Manuel Swartz of Edgartown, whose boatbuilding house is now the Old Sculpin Gallery.

The trip to Edgartown was a formal passage. Adelaide Seager, who lived at the end of North Neck, donned her hat and white gloves and walked to her dock where her captain was waiting in the Seagers' lovely wooden catboat to take her into Edgartown to buy groceries and supplies.

One of the earliest summer people, John J. Jeremiah, built a big Victorian home high on a bluff overlooking Katama Bay and Norton Point that is now the Richard Chasin house. Although I never met him, Mr. Jeremiah was described as tall, gray-haired, dignified, and kindly.

Mr. Jeremiah had a boatman who sailed him into town in his catboat. In case he was threatened with inclement weather, he also had a house and dock in Edgartown on South Water Street. Called the "Chappy House," it is now owned by the Harborside Inn and is still used to house guests of the Inn. When bad weather came or the ferry broke down, Mr. Jeremiah invited Chappy people to stay in his Edgartown house until the storm had abated or the ferry was running again. At one point, he proposed building a bridge from Edgartown to Chappy. (See sidebar page 128.) Fortunately, nothing came of it.

Guvnor Handy

A HORSE NAMED DOLLY

B ill Handy (called "Guvnor" by all) lived on a farmstead near the Chappy five corners off Sampson's Hill Road (now Old Indian Trail). He drove to the ferry in his horse and buggy and left his horse in one of the sheds while he went into town by rowboat to pick up groceries for the summer people.

The Guvnor, who served as the postmaster of Chappaquiddick, also picked up some liquor for himself and enjoyed it mightily on his trip up the road on his return to Chappy. He would fall asleep on the seat of the wagon, and his horse Old Dolly kept going on the appointed rounds, knowing where to stop. A maid or cook appeared, picked up groceries from the wagon, left a list for the next trip, and gave Dolly a slap on the rump. Dolly then went to the next house until they arrived home. By then, Guvnor was usually sober or Dolly would stand patiently in front of the barn until he awoke and took care of her.

Guvnor also took many people in his buggy up Meeting House Hill for Sunday services. Guvnor would sit in the back of the meeting house with Dolly's long driving reins in his hand as she grazed outside. Every now and then in the middle of a prayer or sermon, the Guvnor would say in a loud voice, "Whoa Dolly!" even though she was contentedly eating grass and not interested in moving anywhere.

Dolly's grave is marked by a stone with her name on it, just off the Chasins' driveway.

The most interesting of the houses and docks on North Neck – including those owned by T.Y. Brown (at the gut), the Pinneys', and the Child/Bird families – was the Marshall family's Big Camp.

Small by today's standards the Big Camp had two stories and a distinctive roof with very large gable ends and a continuous roof line that covered the porch. It was started in 1887 and completed in 1904, and seemed large compared to other small summer houses on the outer harbor. The Marshalls had taken advantage of the flat, rolling landscape to create a golf course, which still remains, and a tennis court, the first on Chappy. The Big Camp remains a landmark for those sailing from East Chop to Edgartown.

THERE WERE A FEW OLD CARS BROUGHT TO CHAPPY BY A scow that was pulled by Jimmy Yates in his rowboat, but most summer people walked everywhere, the children barefoot. The winding roads were narrow and sandy, but since there were very few cars, they stayed in fine condition.

There was no phone service until the early 1930s and no electricity until 1934. Both were installed first at the Point, the ferry landing, and gradually progressed up the main road. Electric poles were installed within reach of the Farm House in the late 1930s and electricity spread gradually along the main road to other houses on the island. It took many years to get electricity and phones all the way to Wasque. When telephones came, the party lines provided us sisters with great entertainment. Even though we were told not to, we listened in and sometimes gave ourselves away with our giggles. Then we were severely reprimanded by the people talking on the line.

Without electricity to pump water, we had no plumbing and used hand pumps, kerosene lamps, and outhouses. The first refrigerators after the old wooden iceboxes were powered by kerosene. A few families had a Kohler generator that supplied a limited amount of electricity for refrigeration and eventually water and an indoor bathroom. (Oh joy!)

Outhouses on Chappy were always interesting. Most were "one-holers" usually decorated with pictures cut from

Edo and Babe at Camp "Hate-to-Quit-It" in 1939, which was formerly known as the Gunning Camp.

The outhouse, and the "decorations" pasted on its walls.

magazines and graced with a Sears Roebuck catalog if there was no toilet paper. Two-holers were interesting as they had one regular-sized hole and often one that was smaller for children. The best of all was one we discovered at a house on Katama Bay. It had three holes, large, medium, and small.

ON SUNDAYS DURING THE 1920S AND BEFORE MANY CARS came to Chappy, the summer people drove their horses and buggies to the top of Sampson's Hill, then known as Meeting House Hill, to attend church services. The charming little meeting house had sky-blue walls and white seats in the pews that were trimmed in brightly varnished dark wood.

Meeting House Hill itself had been an important spot in earlier years. It had been used as a semaphore station during the whaling era, and messages were relayed by wooden arms from Nantucket to Chappy and then to the Cape and eventually all the way to Boston. The arms reported the arrival of whaling ships and their cargo, important information for the merchants of Boston to learn as early as possible. Once a semaphore operator got mixed up somewhere along the line, and the message that reached Boston was that a whale ship had arrived in Nantucket with a load of smallpox.

The little church gradually passed out of use, as more people had cars and could go to Edgartown for services, and fewer ministers were willing to come to Chappy to conduct services. The 1938 hurricane did major damage to the Meeting House structure. It didn't take long before it was vandalized and left to the mercy of the elements. The windows were broken, the door was swinging in the wind, and the pews, walls, and ceiling were discolored by the rain. Eventually the building became so decrepit that it was torn down. One of the pews was rescued by Foster Silva, a well-known year-round resident. He gave it to Lee Brown, a summer resident, and the pew is now in the library at the Community Center. The Martha's Vineyard Museum eventually cleared the site and put up a stone

Looking across at Edgartown Point from the Chappy Point and ferry landing in about 1944.

with a plaque commemorating the Meeting House and the semaphore station.

Meeting House Hill was one of the few high areas on the island, which was so flat and open you could see from one side to the other in many places. Several windmills stood on the horizon. The windmill that I remember best was at the Bunkers' house on Katama. Made of wood and called a "Dempster," it was the same sort used all over America's West to pump water for livestock in remote places that had no access to electricity. A large wooden

Chappy's Farms

FOOD FOR ALL

In the early years working farms were an important resource for the summer people. It was difficult to get to town for supplies, and with no refrigeration, preserving food was a problem.

Along with Pimpneymouse, Tom's Neck and Wasque Farms helped provide food to the summer people. Tom's Neck Farm, owned and run by Ben Pease and his wife Annie, had been in the family for many generations. A few sheep still wandered the hills and fields in the 1930s, and it seemed to me that there was always a baby lamb or runt brought up by Mrs. Pease and fed with a baby bottle in the kitchen by the big black stove.

Joe Sequera lived at Wasque Farm and farmed for the Garrett family. He was a short, wiry man who worked hard and produced a prodigious amount of food for the Garretts. A fourth farm, run by Sally Jeffers (see sidebar page 89) rounded out the agricultural offerings on Chappy.

barrel near the top under the windmill blades held the pumped water. If the wind was strong, the wooden barrel would overflow. Even in a calm, the barrel always leaked, and there was nothing more refreshing on a hot day than to ride our horses under the windmill and let the cold water pour over us. The horses liked it as much as we did.

Edo and Hope make a delivery for the
Chappaquiddick Weekly.

Chapter Eight

THE CHAPPAQUIDDICK WEEKLY

IN 1937 MY OLDER SISTER RUTH DECIDED TO START A newspaper. She called it *The Chappaquiddick Weekly,* and she brought it out on Wednesdays to "scoop" the *Vineyard Gazette.*

The Lion's Hotel became our office. With a tiny old Royal typewriter and with two eager fingers each, we typed our stories, mostly about family and friends, dogs, pets, and the Farm.

Ruthie could type a bit better than the rest of us and was the editor. A couple of her friends were part of the staff, and Hope and I were jacks-of-all-trades, the "gofers" ready to do whatever was asked. Occasionally, we called on our mother to be our backup typist, since she was a good typist — and fast.

The first issue, mostly gossip, came out in August of 1937. It was typed on an eight-by-eleven-inch sheet of paper, and we were able to make about six copies at a time with carbon paper.

Carbon paper was a hard way to produce a newspaper, but we stuck with it. We were very proud when we expanded to two pages of news items, riddles, recipes, jokes, a "society" section, and even advertisements (which were free).

We started *The Chappaquiddick Weekly* on August 2, 1937, and charged two cents per copy. When the newspaper expanded to three pages, we added poetry, a women's column, a men's column, a ghost story, and even sports, and upped our rates. We stopped publication each year around the middle of September.

In 1938 the paper expanded to three pages, then four, and we had thirty customers, even off-island ones. For five cents, we would mail the newspaper to them.

Fortunately, the gift of a "hectograph" that year from one of my father's friends greatly increased our printing capabilities after 1937. Now we typed only one copy with a special ribbon and put the result on a jelly-like substance in a shallow rectangular tray. After a few moments you removed the paper, and the print was copied in the jelly. You laid down fresh paper, then picked it up to find the print clearly transferred to the paper. It seemed a miracle.

THE BEST PART OF THE PAPER WAS THE DELIVERY, MADE ON horseback. It was often cold and wet, and, like the mail, went through in all weather. By 1938 we had devised a canvas canopy made from an old sail and attached to our pony cart, so that we and the paper stayed dry. We charged ten

The hectograph, operated by Edo, made duplication of the newspaper easier.

Pimpneymouse Farm

THE CHAPPAQUIDDICK WEEKLY

VOL. 3
NO. 5

July 22, 1939

VOL. 4
NO. 7

THE CHAPPAQUIDDICK WEEKLY

MONDAY
AUGUST 12, 1940

Ferry

On

when

rop

ex

f

*** NEWS ***

DIAMOND RING - CONT. FROM GAZETTE
The diamond
ring that was lost on Tuesday was found on
Friday. The Insurance company sent over a div-
er from New Bedford on Friday morning. He
started at 10 o'clock in the morning and never
found it till two in the afternoon. It was a
very lucky and remarkable thing for him to find
it at all.

MORE

g pheasants
keep
are of
Island.
oose
they

THE CHAPPAQUIDDICK WEEKLY
MONDAY
AUG. 19, 1940

VOL. 4
NO. 8

*** NEWS ***

A RUNAWAY HORSE
Ann Child's horse, Happy, has
been doing a lot of travelling around the island
by himself lately. Last Saturday he was tied to
a tree by the Childs house and desiring to go
somewhere else he pulled up the tree and started
off. He went to Sally Jeffers where Gladys caught
him, but Mrs. Jeffers thinking that he would
appreciate more freedom then he had already had,
let him go again. He finally ended up at the
Welch's where he was caught and put in their
barn, till the Childs called for him.

A POPULAR CAMPING GROUND
More girl scouts were
here to spend the night on South Beach last
Friday. It seems that a different group comes
over here once every two weeks.

EXTRA MAIL LATELY
Jimmy the mailman has been get-
ting very tired this last week carrying wedding
presents to Josephine Barber almost every single
day. Most likely he hopes that there won't be
many more weddings on Chappaquiddick.

ANNUAL DOG SHOW
The Animal Rescue League are
their annual Dog Show next Sunday, August
we hope that every one will

cents per copy for the newspaper by then and expected cash on delivery.

Most of our customers paid us in advance for the whole summer, so we felt an obligation to keep it going, even though some of us would have happily gone sailing instead. By the end of the first summer we had made a profit of $5. When we argued how to divide it and spend it, my father stepped in and "encouraged" us to give it to the MSPCA. This we did, and I found a great satisfaction in helping the animals at the MSPCA Shelter in Edgartown. Miss Foote, who started the shelter, ran it virtually singlehandedly for many years. The seeds of volunteerism were sown then and have influenced my entire life.

Someone gave us a secondhand mimeograph machine in the later years, and this improvement was terrific. It meant only one copy to type, and gave us more time to gather our news. Some of the "news" printed in the final years was about "a bluefish bonanza, catching 228 fish," July 4th fireworks at the Point, and various "weenie roasts."

The variety of news items was eclectic. "Mrs. Dennis," the pig at the farm, was often featured.

One of my favorite *Weekly* stories was about our dog Trixie, who inadvertently got locked into one of the old buildings at the Dike. Another story in the "Social News" had told about a visit to Mrs. Barber's house on Menaca Hill from her friend Mrs. Francis Peabody Magoon of Boston. At ages 9, 11, and 13 years old, we thought that was the funniest name we had ever heard. Another headline read, "Accident at Hair Pin Turn." and related how the farm truck and another vehicle had hit each other; fortunately, we reported, no one was injured.

Even sailing was reported in the *Weekly*. The International America's Cup races in the 1930s were sailed in J Boats. They were immense boats, much larger than anything seen around here today, well over 100 feet long. Their spinnakers were as big as blimps. We reported that the "Cup Defenders and a 3-Masted Square Rigger" were anchored off the Beach Club in 1937.

Sally Jeffers got a feature story in the *Weekly* that year because the Astors and Vanderbilts from their twelve-meter yachts came to Chappaquiddick for her famous clambake.

THE PAPER CONTINUED FOR FIVE YEARS AND FINALLY stopped in 1941 because of World War II. Our last issue showed that our rudimentary efforts had turned into a much more professional-looking journal. Every issue of those four years is still stored in the Farm House.

We did have a moment of glory in the final issue in 1941 when my sister, Ruth, the editor, wrote an editorial asking that the Town of Edgartown not pave the Chappy Road. We liked it dirt because we enjoyed going barefoot in the sand. Even though our plea failed, the editorial was reprinted in the *Vineyard Gazette* and then picked up by *The New York Times*.

Ending publication of the *Weekly* was sad, but we were ready to move on to other efforts. The next generation pro-

Edo practices her two-fingered pecking at the typewriter to put out the newspaper.

duced other, more sophisticated newspapers on Chappy. The *Chappy Chronicles*, created by Trip Barnes and Liz Franzen, was a success for a short time in the 1950s. Not to be outdone, Vance Packard and John Seibel published *Chappy Chatter*, ostensibly to "put Tripp and Liz out of business."

My daughter, Hatsy Potter, created the *Chappy Chit Chat* and, with the help of Eric Gostenhofer and Cynthia Plumb (now Hubbard) and others, they kept it going for two years in 1964 and 1965. They interviewed some old timers and had wonderful stories in the *Chit Chat* about early Chappaquiddick. Finally my son, Stephen, tried his hand and continued the *Chit Chat* for another summer, until the teenagers lost interest as other things took up their time.

The City of Chappaquiddick ferry, with Tony Bettencourt at the helm, moves toward Edgartown.

Chapter Nine

GETTING FROM HERE TO THERE

THE CHAPPAQUIDDICK FERRIES HAVE ALWAYS BEEN AN integral part of our history.

The first ferries were rowboats, with the first one reported as early as 1812. The first ferryman I heard about, from older summer people, was Walstein Osborn, called Steen. He rowed across the harbor with a bit of help from his passengers. Steen was mostly blind, but he knew the tides, currents, and the effects of the wind so well that he could always find his way. Once in a while, if need be, Steen's passengers told him which oar to pull harder on to reach their destination.

When people wanted to bring their animals across, they tied a halter rope to the rowboat, and Steen started rowing. Onlookers "persuaded the animal from behind," usually by twisting the animal's tail around toward the front, and the horse or cow had no choice but to swim.

Jimmy Yates, the next rowboat captain, took over from Steen in 1920 and charged people six cents. He made the transportation of animals easier by towing a small, flat-bottomed scow behind his rowboat. At that time, Katama Bay was closed to the ocean behind a strong barrier beach. There was no cut in the beach and very little current near the ferry crossing. Towing a small but heavy barge with only oar power was a hard but not impossible trip.

Passengers rang a bell on either ferry landing to get Jimmy Yates's attention and service. Life on the waterfront in the late 1920s when my father first bought the land on Chappy was filled with practical jokes, and the bell played a cameo role in at least one of them: Some of the waterfront hangers-on tied a rope to the bottom stern of Jimmy Yates's boat and the other end to a stanchion on shore. They

The horse Lucille arrives by ferry from Seven Gates Farm to live on Chappy. (Photo Clara Dinsmore)

weighted the rope down in the middle so that it wasn't visible above water. They had arranged to have someone on Chappy ring the big bell for Jimmy to pick them up. Jimmy started rowing from the Edgartown side, and he rowed and rowed and rowed. Finally someone retrieved the bell ringer on Chappy and Jimmy gave up and returned to Edgartown shaking his head, to tell the assembled perpetrators, "That was the hardest row I have ever had."

Jimmy Yates's rowboat gave way in 1929 to Tony Bettencourt, who built and towed a scow with his motorboat, *Sleepy*. It could take only one car, but that was a dramatic improvement over oars. Tony got a charter from the county commissioners to "operate the passenger launch called *Sleepy* and to tow a 20 by 8 foot scow once or twice a week for the transporting of a Model T, small pickups, or horse drawn carts."

The first motorized scow was built by Manuel Swartz for Tony in 1934. It was only thirty-six feet long, a little more than half the size of the largest ferry now, which is sixty-five feet long. Named the *City of Chappaquiddick* by *Vineyard Gazette* reporter Joe Allen, it was built on Chappy Point upside down (the easiest way) and turned over and launched for Tony by a friend who happened to have a crane on Chappy to build the jetties at Cape Pogue.

The *City of Chappaquiddick* was not a double-ender like the present ferries. The cars drove on frontwards, and Tony backed the scow out of the slip, turned around in a large semicircle, and headed for Chappy. There the cars backed off on two planks. Tony then backed out from the

Cars line up to take the Chappy ferry across in a photo in 1941.

Chappy side, turned around, and the process would be repeated on the Edgartown side.

Tony had no regular hours, and you had to make arrangements to have him take you across if he wasn't at the landing. Usually a call to Laura Paul, the telephone operator in Edgartown for many years, would find Tony. Laura Paul knew everyone in town and usually where they were; when my father called from Marblehead to talk to his farmer, Frank Drake, Laura Paul would tell him that Frank was at so-and-so's-house and ask if he wanted to be connected there.

Tony's young nephew, Foster Silva, invented a new sport when he was young. Riding a bicycle, he would start at the top of the hill in front of the library and race down Daggett Street toward the ferry as fast as he could go, hit one of the two narrow board ramps at full speed, and hope he was on target. If he was, he reached the end of the ferry, still at full speed, and went flying off into the water, landing with an enormous splash and with cheers from onlookers.

This practice was eventually banned, though many years later a young Edgartown boy named Peter Wells – who in 2008 bought the Chappy ferry – revived the sport temporarily. There is a great home video of Peter pedaling furiously toward the ferry and arcing into the air as he and his bicycle went off the end of the ferry on the Chappy side with an enormous splash and lots of cheers from the onlookers. A rope with a float was attached to the bicycle to prevent it sinking to the bottom for good.

THE CHAPPY FERRY WAS NOT WITHOUT ITS DRAMA. IN 1938 a seaplane came in to make a landing in the harbor from the direction of the lighthouse. The next thing anyone knew, the seaplane was headed right for the Chappy ferry as the ferry came out of the Edgartown slip.

A truck driver on board the ferry, as well as several passengers, jumped into the water to save themselves. One woman who couldn't swim clung to the corner of the ferry as the plane's wing hit the truck and nose-dived into the water on the far side of the ferry. The truck tipped over but came to rest on the ferry's railing and did not go into the water. The plane stayed afloat long enough for the plane's passengers and pilot to be rescued before it sank. By great good fortune a Coast Guard vessel was tied

The Great Expanse

WHY NOT A BRIDGE?

J ohn J. Jeremiah, a summer person who built a big Victorian summer house on the bluff overlooking Katama Bay, thought he could improve access to Chappy in the 1920s. He placed an article in a Town Meeting warrant asking the Town to spend $100,000 to build a bridge from Chappy to Edgartown.

Designed to cross the harbor at its narrowest point down harbor, it would have spanned Katama Bay. Plans for this substantial structure can be seen in detail at the Chappy Community Center.

The selling point was that it would bring more summer people to "beautiful Chappaquiddick and all its wonderful beaches and waterfront properties and it would be an economic boost to the Town of Edgartown." Fortunately, the bridge plans were not approved at town meeting, and our little island of Chappaquiddick remained a rural haven for self-sufficient people who sought peace and quiet.

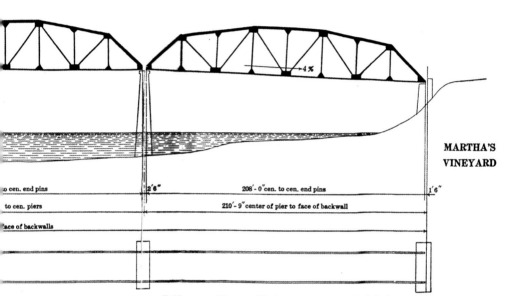

MARTHA'S
VINEYARD

—4 %

:o cen. end pins   2′ 6″   208′ - 0″ cen. to cen. end pins   1′ 6″

to cen. piers   210′ - 9″ center of pier to face of backwall

ace of backwalls

Bridge over Edgarton Harbor to Chappaquiddick Is′d

3-Thro Riveted Truss Highway Spans, 208′-0″ cen. to cen. end pins

Scale: $\frac{1}{50}'' = 1'\text{-}0''$

American Bridge Company
New York Office
30 Church St., Oct. 22, 1924
DRAWING NO. B-8257

Inquiry No. E-83192-10

Rev. Jan. 27, 1925

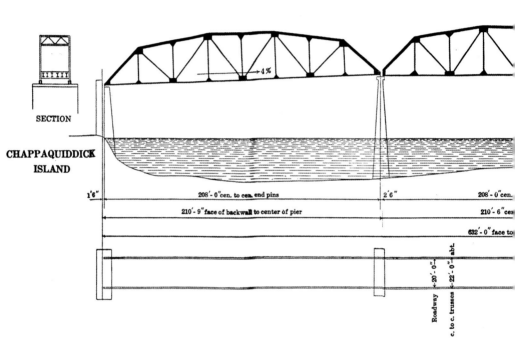

SECTION

CHAPPAQUIDDICK
ISLAND

1'6" | 208'- 0" cen. to cen. end pins | 2'6" | 208'- 0" cen.

210'- 9" face of backwall to center of pier | 210'- 6" cen

632'- 0" face to

Roadway 20' - 0"

c. to c. trusses 22' - 0" abt.

→ 4 %

up to the Steamboat Dock (now Memorial Wharf), and its crew made quick work of picking up the wet ferry and plane passengers.

Tony always took care of what he called his Chappy "children," both young and old, making sure they could get home to and from Edgartown no matter the inconvenience to him. In the late thirties, a group of teenagers from Chappy had been invited to a dance at the Edgartown Yacht Club. Tony took them to Edgartown and told them to be back by 11 p.m., and he would return them to Chappy.

When the teens were late, Tony drove his ferry from the slip on the Edgartown side where he was patiently waiting to the Yacht Club. He tied up to the Yacht Club dock and appeared on the dance floor, announcing in a loud voice, "C'mon, children, I'm taking you home."

MY MOTHER NEVER FORGOT A TRIP FROM EDGARTOWN when the rudder became disabled and the ferry began drifting out of the harbor and toward points north on a falling tide. At that time the main current ran closer to the lighthouse and straight out to Nantucket Sound.

Tony assessed the problem and said, as he so often did in unusual situations, and with his usual equanimity, "Don't worry, children, I will get you back to Chappy." He tied a rope onto a bucket and threw the bucket over the stern, holding onto the rope and walking from one corner of the stern to the other to guide the ferry. Each time the ferry would turn in the direction of the pull, and Tony skillfully steered the ferry back toward the slip.

The winter of 1947 had an unusually long spell of bitter cold, with the Edgartown harbor frozen. I was newly married, and my husband, Bob, was a student at Harvard University. We had invited two graduate-student friends to spend New Year's with us and now faced the chance we couldn't get to the Woods' Hole ferry for one of the few trips a day at that time of year. It seemed impossible, but we talked to Tony, who assured us he could get us to the ferry despite what was going to have to be a very early crossing over the ice from Chappy to Edgartown, in the dark, well before dawn.

Saltwater ice is notoriously treacherous. It never freezes evenly and has soft, mushy spots which don't harden. We met Tony at the shore at 5 a.m., and followed him onto the ice. Six of us, including my mother, were strung out behind him at a safe distance, holding onto a sturdy rope. If one person fell in, the person in front or behind could pull him out.

Tony had an axe in his hand, and as he walked slowly ahead, he dropped the axe blade onto the ice in front of him. If the axe bounced off solid ice, Tony kept going. If the axe went through the ice or if the ice was mushy, he would turn and take another route. Slowly and silently, often holding our breath and with pounding hearts, we continued in this manner.

When we finally made it to Edgartown, I asked, "How do we get to Vineyard Haven?" No taxis waited for us in those days. Tony, of course, had the answer. He had left an

Captain Tony Bettencourt aboard his ferry City of Chappaquiddick.

old car in Edgartown. All six of us piled in. After sputtering for a few nervous moments, the old car started, but it only would run in second gear. The ride to Vineyard Haven was slow and exceedingly noisy, but we made it to the ferry on time.

TONY SOLD THE FERRY BUSINESS TO HIS NEPHEW, FOSTER Silva, in 1949 but kept the *City of Chappaquiddick*. For many years he used it to take people fishing or on sightseeing tours around the harbor. It ended up at Edgartown Marine, which

Tony Bettencourt

FERRYBOAT CAPTAIN

E veryone's favorite person on the island was Tony Bettencourt, otherwise known as Cap because he ran the ferry or Midge because of his short stature.

Tony lived with his family in the farmhouse known as Whale Jaw Farm across from the present Chappy store. He had dragged an enormous whale jawbone up from the beach and put it at the beginning of his driveway, where it still stands. Later, Tony built the Dyke House near the Dike Bridge, giving it the name that has lasted through several owners.

Tony ran the City of Chappaquiddick, *the first motorized scow across the channel, on an informal basis. There was no schedule, and gardening or rabbit hunting might mean his passengers had to wait. After the 1938 hurricane damaged the buildings on Chappy Point, Tony built a ferry house with windows, a door, and a porch. There were two benches inside where you retreated during bad weather for the wait. Sometimes we were cheered by the peeping of baby chicks that Tony kept in the ferry house because it had electricity to keep his brooder warm.

He was always hospitable and had what seemed like an endless supply of wine he made from Chappy grapes. In later years we would sing Christmas carols around the island from door to door, and Tony's was always the last and best stop. Tony's wine and his wife Edna's goodies were special.*

He loved rabbit hunting and had a series of beagles, each one named Molly. They were scrawny little things that Tony always claimed could get through the green brier on Chappy better than larger dogs. This was proven true when a man named Jimmy Jones brought his fancy pack of beagles from New Jersey, arriving on Chappy in full regalia – green jackets with brass buttons, small horns to call the dogs, and whips to control them.

The New Jersey dogs immediately attacked Molly, who had to be rescued and shut in Tony's car for protection. However, she wasn't shut in for long because the fancy beagles from New Jersey met up with the green brier and turned tail and ran for their cages, yipping in pain. Molly was let out and was immediately onto a rabbit. That was the last time Jimmy Jones brought his fancy pack to Chappy.

has since built a scaled-down replica of it for the July 4th parade in Edgartown.

When Foster bought the ferry business from Tony, the Town gave Foster eleven days to build a new ferry in order to keep the franchise. No one thought it could be done, but Captain Sam Norton, who lived in the house next to Manuel Swartz's boat shop in Edgartown, took on the task. He was well known for house moving and other difficult

The Chappy ferry landing. The planks in the foreground were to help get cars and livestock onto the boat.

tasks but never anything like this. He built the ferry upside down and turned it over to launch it.

It was finished by midnight on the eleventh day and in the water and operating at the next high tide. The ferry was rightfully named *On Time.*

Two more *On Time*s have since been built, both by Jerry Grant, who ran the ferry for more than twenty years. The first one, *On Time II,* was built in Jerry's backyard,

without a marine architect. Tony Bettencourt often stopped by to keep track of the progress, frequently shaking his head and saying that it wouldn't work. But Jerry was stubborn and wanted to do it his own way. He put a keel on the bottom instead of having a flat bottom like most scows, thinking it would make it more stable and hold a straighter course.

Jerry's new ferry was moved overland and launched at State Beach. When it hit the water, the keel scraped the bottom. The men launching it finally got it out deep enough to float, but to their surprise it floated so high that the propeller and rudder didn't touch the water. To bring it down to the right level Jerry put several tons of cement blocks in the bilge. It has remained that way ever since, although current ferry owner Peter Wells confessed to me that Jerry had let him take some cement blocks out to build the chimney of Peter's house on Chappy.

Jerry Grant built the *On Time III* in his backyard as well, but this time, it had a flat bottom and has been a real workhorse.

In 1970, when my husband and I spent our first full winter on Chappy, only thirty-two people lived here year-round. With so few winter residents and so little use of the ferry, there was no need to run the ferry all day. The schedule for trips during the week was from 8 to 11 a.m. and from 3 to 6 p.m. Between 11 and 3 there were no trips.

The ferry house in Jerry's day was a real house with a door, front porch, and benches inside. It was damaged in one of the later hurricanes and replaced with the present smaller version nearer the slip so that you had a shorter distance to walk in rain and wind.

The old structure was a welcome place for the frequent long waits. Over one of the benches was a drawing and message that read, *"This bench is dedicated to those who died waiting for the three o'clock ferry."*

Artie West and Edo, looking for bluefish in July 1938.

Chapter Ten

MESSING ABOUT IN BOATS

BOTH MY PARENTS LOVED THE WATER, AND WERE ADEPT and intense sailors. Both had raced boats in Marblehead, and both transferred their interests, though in different ways, to the waters around Chappy.

Edgartown Harbor was a special place, known in the 1930s as one of the best and most beautiful harbors to be found anywhere. That was before it became crowded with more motorboats than sailboats, and when it was not uncommon to see large boats coming into the harbor under full sail. It also was a time when, with no opening in South Beach, the harbor was a calm oasis compared to today with its strong currents.

The star of the local fleet, as well as up and down the East Coast, was the 116-foot sailing yawl *Manxman*. She was as large as a "J Boat," which was one of the largest racing craft in the 1930s and the class of boats used in the America's

From left to right, Mae West, *a sailing dinghy; a kayak; and* Gadget *were part of the Welch family fleet.*

Cup races. *Manxman* had a thirteen-foot draft and a twenty-foot beam when it was built in 1927. With a black hull, shiny and sleek, and a long narrow bow, she was a breathtaking sight.

Manxman was originally designed as a sloop with a single towering mast. After an accident that broke off the top of the mast, she was rerigged as a yawl and was, at that time, the largest yawl in the world. She was skippered by Samuel B. Norton – Captain Sam – who was born and brought up in Edgartown on the waterfront when the harbor was a commercial fishing center.

Captain Sam prided himself on sailing into Edgartown Harbor under full sail, with no engine running. He set a course on the port tack from the red nun, the last government buoy, just outside the harbor. At maximum speed, with a good southwest wind blowing, *Manxman* headed straight on what looked like a collision course for the Steamboat Dock, now known as Memorial Wharf. Her white bow wave contrasted with her gleaming black hull as she stormed along with all sails set. It was an awesome sight and an even more awesome performance by a very able captain.

There were lots of large sailing yachts in the 1930s before World War II. When the America's Cup racing J Boats arrived in 1937, all in the 120-foot range, they moored in Edgartown's outer harbor with their huge tenders. At night with their riding lights, it looked like a cityscape.

MY FATHER'S OWN BOAT, *WALRUS*, WAS A TRANSITION FROM his sailing days to his motorboat and fishing days. Charlie enjoyed the *Walrus* greatly, even though she was very different from the sleek racing boats he had captained in international waters. She was sturdy and seaworthy with a bluff bow and a squared stern.

Swordfishing was a popular sport as well as a commercial enterprise in the 1930s, and *Walrus* was perfect for it. She had both port and starboard ratlines leading up to two stands for the lookouts and a crow's nest at the very top of the mast. When a swordfish was spotted, usually lazing in the sun at the surface, the harpooner, usually Roy Willoughby from Edgartown, took his place in the pulpit on the bow of the boat.

My father would ease the *Walrus* up to the fish. Once the fish was harpooned, the crew, usually Frank Drake and Leon (Jiggs) Easterbrooks, clambered into the dory, picked up the buoy, and hauled in the fish, bringing it alongside *Walrus* where it was slaughtered and stored on ice.

My father's next boat, *Gadget,* was a fast, narrow boat somewhat like the lobster boats in Maine. She was long and sleek and painted white with a tan canvas spray protector. *Gadget* turned heads when she went by. Her low and narrow stern and overall shape were innovative, and she was fast: *Gadget* could get to the fishing grounds off Wasque quickly, usually ahead of everyone else. The *Chappaquiddick Weekly* had headlines one week reporting "Bluefish Bonanza: 228 bluefish caught by Mr. Welch and Artie West."

My mother was also a very keen and successful skipper. She spent many years sailing all over New England. In Edgartown she was part of an all-female crew, skippered by Clare Dinsmore of Edgartown, who won the Women's Nationals called the Adams Cup.

In 1939 she had the use of *Yankee,* a new and fast boat that was the beginning of a new class of boats. Although sailing with her was always a delight, sometimes neither my mother's experience and skill nor *Yankee* made the trips easy. Once when she was trying to pick up the mooring near the lighthouse in Edgartown, the wind was blowing strongly from the southwest, and the current, shooting straight in the harbor from the northeast, under an open bridge between the lighthouse and the Harborview Hotel, was even stronger.

Manxman, *captained by Sam Norton of Edgartown, docked in Edgartown.*

She tried five times to shoot the mooring, head to wind, but the current would push *Yankee* right on by. I was the inexperienced young crew and feared we would be sailing around all night until the tide turned. Finally she approached the mooring downwind the wrong way and against the tide, making the perfect approach for me to pick up the mooring while she hastily took down the sails. I was in awe of her capabilities – that sort of sailing isn't taught in the books. It took thought and skilled sailboat handling.

I INHERITED MY LOVE OF SAILING FROM BOTH MY PARENTS.

We were not members of the Edgartown Yacht Club, so I couldn't participate in club races. However, I discovered I

Yankee under sail in 1938, skippered by Ruth Welch, Edo's mother.

Ben Cromwell and Ike Pease
HERMITS AND LONERS

T hey say that loners like to live on islands, and that was true of Ben Cromwell and Ike Pease. They couldn't have picked a more remote spot than East Beach and Cape Pogue in the 1930s.

Ben Cromwell lived in a shack in the cedars just north of the Dyke Bridge. Inside, the walls were lined with books. Ben loved to fish. In his slippers, when the fish were running, he padded out to East Beach and threw a line with the rest of the fishermen, heaving and hauling a heavy line and lure with no rod and reel.

Rumor had it that he had dropped out of MIT. He cherished his books and enjoyed living there alone. Sadly his demise came when the shack caught fire, and both he and his books were burned.

Our island's other hermit, Ike Pease lived in a shack near Cape Pogue lighthouse. A number of small houses were occupied there, during the summers in the 1930s, before World War II came and prohibited nonmilitary people from inhabiting or trespassing on the land near the lighthouse.

Ike was the only one who lived at Cape Pogue year round. During the summer, he rowed back and forth to Edgartown for supplies for himself, for a tea room that was there for many years, and for others living near the lighthouse. He would often return after dark and through fierce weather. He made a modest living by caretaking the summer houses and supported himself by fishing, shell fishing, hunting, and picking berries.

They were both one-of-a-kind people who lived life just the way they wanted it.

Edo Potter, at ease at the helm.

could be a crew for a Yacht Club member. I wasn't allowed to touch the tiller but could busy myself with the sails. The class of boats for the young at that time was called a Beach Boat, built by the catboat designer Manuel Swartz in his boat shed near the Chappy ferry landing. A small one-design class, Beach Boats had a mainsail and a jib, the small sail in front of the mainsail.

For several summers I crewed in a Beach Boat for anyone who would have me and read and studied anything I could get my hands on about sailing and racing. Eventually I was asked to crew on bigger racing boats, and there were times when I was allowed to skipper.

This interest and these experiences led to many years of cruising, but one of the greatest sails in my memory happened when I was about twelve. A friend of my father's owned a lovely large black yawl, the *Jane Dore*. He often came into Edgartown Harbor with his family and visited us at the Farm. At the end of the summer, he would return to his homeport in Connecticut. When I was twelve, he invited me to accompany them home.

Off Narragansett Bay, the weather was perfect, and a southeast wind was pushing us along from the rear. The family put up all six sails, including the spinnaker. They asked me to take the helm, then all disappeared below deck, leaving me alone topsides, telling me to call them if I needed help. I was in my glory, too young to realize that it was a somewhat unusual sight to see this big yawl with no one on deck except a freckle-faced twelve-year-old at the helm.

Chapter Eleven

WASQUE: THE MOST BEAUTIFUL PLACE IN THE WORLD

WASQUE, THE SOUTHEASTERLY END OF CHAPPAQUID-dick, was – and is today — astonishingly beautiful. In the 1930s, it had wide-open grasslands with no pines or other trees except some gnarled and wind-twisted oaks near Wasque Point that had been able to withstand the harsh and windy climate. The grasses, flowers, and small shrubs made a mosaic of color that was different in every season.

Nothing impeded the view of the water on three sides of Wasque. Completely open from the house with the tower that still stands to the ocean beach and from Katama Bay to Poucha Pond, you were always reminded by the water views that Chappy was an island. On a clear day, you could see to Nantucket, and it seemed to us almost to Spain.

The land mass of Wasque was much larger in the early 1930s. During the 1938 hurricane, about a quarter of a mile of the beach area disappeared, including a road where my mother liked to drive to enjoy the ocean view and waves. (See Chapter 12 on the 1938 hurricane.) Over 200 acres have disappeared into the sea since the 1800s, and over 700 feet since 2007.

THE COLORS OF WASQUE SEEMED EVER-CHANGING. IN THE spring the new grass was a vivid green; the trailing arbutus, known locally as mayflowers, added their delicate pink and

Looking from Wasque to East Beach.

white; the later leaves of the barberry were a dark green, and in the fall the rosy reds and rusts of the berry bushes made a glorious finale. From a distance, it looked like a magic carpet.

The land was filled with low bush blueberries, densely laden with small flavorful wild berries, and in July we filled buckets for pies, blueberry grunt, bead puddings, pancakes, and all sorts of wonderful food; without a freezer, they had to be used up quickly.

Wasque appeared completely untrammeled. By the 1930s the sheep that had been pastured there were gone,

and only small animals like rabbits and voles scurried through the brush and grasses. Marsh hawks (now called harriers) cruised overhead, gracefully slipping and tilting on the air currents.

It seemed that Wasque had never been occupied by man, although at one time a good-sized settlement of Indians and whites lived there to be near the fishing grounds. All signs of them had gone; no houses, no wigwams (called wetus by the Indians), no fences. Three narrow trails through the grass and low shrubs marked the best way to get to the south side of Wasque, to Wasque Point or to Poucha Pond. All year the gray green of the reindeer moss (actually a lichen) punctuated the grassland, crinkling and crackling underfoot as you walked over the open landscape.

WHEN WE WERE YOUNG, WASQUE WAS A FAVORITE PLACE TO ride. On horseback we had a vantage point and an overall view of this spectacular landscape. We rode through blowing clumps of "bunchgrass" that looked like ballerinas taking a bow.

Fortunately, no burrowing animals like woodchucks or gophers lived on Chappy, making it safe to gallop across the smooth, mostly flat and open terrain. We galloped at top speed and pulled up short, as breathless with the thrill as the horses were with their enthusiastic exertion.

The tower on the Weston house was, I believe, built by the family of an elderly woman who had grown too old to go to the beach. I have been told that she was carried up to the tower and spent hours enjoying a 360-degree view.

During World War II, when gas was rationed and could only be used for essentials such as for farming and food shopping, we were lucky to have horses.

My father suggested picnicking at Wasque during the war. He hitched up the black, double-seated Democrat Wagon behind Lucille, a driving as well as a riding horse, and the pony cart behind Babe to take us to Wasque every nice Sunday during the war. My mother made a picnic lunch, stashed it under the rear seat of the so-called Democrat Wagon, and off we went. My father drove with my mother seated beside him. One of the three girls sat in the back seat. The other two sisters drove along behind with Babe in her small wooden cart.

We argued about who would be in Babe's two-wheeled cart. In it, we felt independent, even though we were only allowed to follow and not to lead. We even tried to include all three of us behind Babe, hitching the little red wagon (that every family seemed to have) to the back of Babe's cart and dragging it along on its small, hard, rubber wheels. Since it had no springs, it jolted over the bumps and stones, hard enough to "shake your teeth out," as my father used to say.

Hopie, the youngest sister, was relegated to the red wagon. She was the smallest and lightest. That arrangement didn't last long because, even with a pillow, the red wagon was too uncomfortable. Hopie finally decided that she preferred the Democrat Wagon with its black leather cushions and its strong metal springs. Compared to the red wagon and even the pony cart, it was a luxurious ride.

My father put up two sturdy hitching posts near the beach where the swimming beach parking is now. Even after the war, they stood like beacons until the 1954 hurricane washed them and a large area of land away.

During the war the Wasque beaches were deserted except for an occasional Coast Guardsman, walking his lonely patrol. We felt we were on a deserted island. We weren't allowed to swim because in the 1940s surf was considered dangerous, and the beach dropped off steeply into the water.

We spent a lot of time at Wasque, not just on the land but on the beaches, marveling at our discoveries. Palm trees were always a great find, and bottles with notes in them were best of all.

One of the attractions to Wasque for us was the Blue Rock. An unusually large rock for that area, which is mostly sand, it had an intriguing history as told by Joseph Chase Allen in his book, *Tales and Trails of Martha's Vineyard*.

According to the story, Captain Kidd moored off Wasque and had two crewmen row him ashore, hauled his treasure up the slope from Poucha Pond to the Blue Rock, and dug a big hole next to it to hide his treasure. At that point he killed both crewmen and buried them with the treasure to ensure secrecy.

What intrigued us was the signs of digging around it. Even more strange were the broken shovels and abandoned digging tools that were lying around. They looked old and rusty and as if someone had left in a hurry.

When Wasque was totally open with sheep-sheared grass, you could see all the way to Katama from the Blue Rock. Several reports from Katama claimed that a blue light had been seen hovering over the rock. We took our turns digging at the rock as others had before us, convinced the story about Captain Kidd was true. We spent a lot of time there, thinking we surely would find the treasure. But we were certain to never be caught there at dusk or after dark. We were convinced there were pirate ghosts around.

WASQUE'S BEAUTY HAD ALWAYS ATTRACTED PEOPLE WITH big plans. In the late 1890s a development called Wasque by the Sea was planned. A railroad was proposed from Oak Bluffs to Edgartown and ultimately to Chappy, on a trestle across the Katama Bay beach. It would then cross Wasque and go all the way to Cape Pogue along East Beach to the lighthouse, and area which had much more acreage than at present.

Plans for the development at both Cape Pogue and Wasque were created by Maude Ayer of Woburn in 1913. The plan for Wasque, called Chappaquiddick by the Sea, had 775 house lots, each on a 10,000-square-foot lot laid out like a grid with a pattern for "streets, avenues, parks, clubhouses, and docking facilities for yachts." Each house had to cost at least $750 when built. Miss Ayer had purchased the land in 1909 from the Pease family, who had used it as a sheep pasture. By 1914 a few lots were sold, but during later years of poor economic times, not a single lot

Rum Runner Lady
AN ISLAND MYSTERY

🐭

I never knew her name, but I heard many stories about the
Rum Runner lady. She lived in a little cottage overlooking a
marsh, a salt pond, and Katama Bay. The cottage was hugged by
large old lilac bushes.

When my sisters and I discovered the cottage and peeked in
the windows, it had been empty for many years, but was still
intact. Its gray weathered shingles blended with the surrounding
low hills, and it seemed to be tucked away safely in its own
green hollow. We could still see signs where a garden had been
planted and carefully tended, but the fields around the house,
that had probably fed a cow or two, were beginning to grow up
into cedars.

The story that I heard was that rum runners brought their
cargo into Katama Bay during Prohibition. They met up with
the crew of a large boat far off the coast. On the darkest night,
with no moon, the rum runners flashed a light to tell the Rum
Runner lady of their presence in Katama Bay. She, in turn,
would put a lamp in her window to say that it was safe to
come ashore. What happened next, I never heard, but it was a
successful enterprise that went on for many years until the end
of Prohibition.

sold. Eventually, her executor sold the remaining lots in their entirety.

Development plans for Cape Pogue showed small lots and a large hotel but that, too, was never built. It was to have been called Country Club Estates.

Fortunately for later generations, the Depression had stopped the development and allowed Charles Sumner Bird and Oliver Filley, two Chappy summer residents, to purchase most of the land from the Dike Bridge to Cape Pogue Gut and donate it to The Trustees of Reservations (TTOR) in 1959. This was the first Trustees property on Martha's Vineyard and has been a wonderful boon to all who live here.

In 1966 the Seward family of Dennis, Massachusetts, owned most of Wasque except the Point, which had been bought by Curtis Nye Smith for a hunting camp. A few small lots overlooking Katama Bay had been purchased, but were not built on for many years. Chappy residents formed the local committee for the Trustees and in December 1967 the Wasque Point Trust purchased Wasque in five units and subsequently sold each parcel to the Trustees. The committee consisted of Oliver Filley, Lee Brown, Russell Stearns, and Mary Wakeman. They purchased Wasque for $250,000 and raised the money and an additional amount for an endowment within a year.

Without these actions, the open, beautiful views of the Wasque of my childhood would have disappeared.

A defused bomb, a life jacket, and a cannon found on Chappy in 1944 were visible reminders of how close the war was.

Chapter Twelve

A HURRICANE AND A WAR

LTHOUGH CHAPPY SEEMED ISOLATED AND SAFE, IT could not avoid the intrusions of both nature and man. The first, a hurricane in 1938, beyond anything ever seen, shook the island but allowed it to escape without major damage; the other, World War II, left Chappaquiddick dramatically changed.

HURRICANES AND TROPICAL STORMS WEREN'T NEW TO THE Vineyard. A storm in 1884, which sank the *City of Columbus* off Gay Head with a tragic loss of over one hundred lives, was memorable.

Yet this late September storm in 1938 was far beyond anyone's memory.

It was spawned in Africa, crossed the South Atlantic, and passed over Florida. In these early days of weather forecasting, weather stations were few and far between. One new young forecaster in Florida suggested the storm might head for New England, but his more experienced cohorts scoffed at him. When the forecasters finally realized what was happening, the storm was hurtling straight toward New England, an unusual path for an Atlantic hurricane, and it was too late to give any warning.

The storm came on September 21, a Wednesday, and the day that the *Chappaquiddick Weekly* was delivered. It was a lovely, still morning, and we had started off early on our

usual rounds, delivering the paper in our pony cart, with Hopie sitting in the little red wagon tied to the back. We first headed toward the ferry, then to North Neck, and ended up near Wasque, where there were only a few houses, before heading home. By then the southerly sky appeared gray and threatening, with a yellowish hue. The clouds moved in at great speed, and the sound of the surf was awesome.

As we turned for home, the wind piped up, as intermittent rain and gusts of wind assaulted our pony cart from the rear.

High waters and flat grasses, the aftermath of the hurricane of 1938. Caleb's Pond overflowed into the outer harbor during the storm. Menaca Hill is in the distance.

Babe, the pony, was nervous and happy to move along toward home. All went well until we turned north to take our shortcut along what we then called the Turnbull trail, crossing Wasque Farm. In 1938 there were no trees between Wasque Farm and Poucha Pond. It was flat grassland, some of the flattest on Chappy. The southeast wind funneled across the fields between the hills of Wasque and the scrub oak woods to the north, grabbing the canopy on Babe's cart that we had jerry-rigged to help keep us dry during our deliveries. The wind kept trying to tip the cart over or lift us into the air.

The heavy canvas of the canopy finally ripped with a tremendous noise, scaring Babe, who raced for home as fast as she could possibly go. We hung on for dear life, praying that we wouldn't hit a tree and with Hope clinging to the little wagon behind us. We made it through the woods and back to the barn in one piece with our hearts pounding and Babe in a cold sweat.

That was the beginning of a very long day, the early part of the storm. We were on the east side of the hurricane, which meant that it wasn't as severe here as it was in Long Island, Connecticut, Rhode Island, and New Bedford.

When we got back to the farm we found our father about to drive a neighbor, Artie West, back to Artie's hunting camp, which was close to Katama Bay at Wasque. It was customary, in bad storms and unusually high tides, for Artie to put the mattress from the bottom bunk in his camp up on the top bunk to avoid getting it wet if the tide was going to be especially high.

My father parked at the high point in the road, and we watched Artie walk down the hill to his camp near the shore. It was blowing hard by then, and the waves striking South Beach at Norton Point were immense, washing over the highest dunes. Artie disappeared inside the camp just as a huge wave came over South Beach, engulfing Katama Bay and heading straight for the camp. To our astonishment the water picked up the camp, carried it up the hill, and grounded it like a beached whale a few yards from where we were watching. Artie walked out of his door, apparently unperturbed, waded through some water, and stepped onto dry land next to us.

Once we'd retrieved Artie, my father decided to check on *Gadget*, which was moored in the harbor. We headed

Artie West's camp at Wasque was typical of the small structures built near the beaches in the 1930s and 1940s.

for what is now the Chappy ferry landing, and got only to the top of the hill before Caleb's Pond when we were awed by the sight of water over the road as far as we could see. The only dry land visible was the top of Menaca Hill. Tony Bettencourt, the ferry owner at that time, had run for his life when he saw a wall of water coming toward him from Katama Bay and only just made it as the wave was swirling around his legs. In the wind-driven rain you could barely see what was left of the Beach Club or any other structures along there.

Standing on the hill, trying to make out what was happening, the wind was so strong that it could easily have blown us over if we didn't hang on to the car.

THE STORM WAS DEADLY. STRIKING IN NEW ENGLAND AND New York, it killed or injured almost 1,500 people. Almost 20,000 homes, cottages, and farms were either destroyed or damaged. Two million fishing boats, equipment, docks, and shore stations were damaged or destroyed. Seven hundred fifty thousand chickens were killed. More than two billion trees were destroyed.

Areas of Martha's Vineyard were leveled. Menemsha lost dozens of buildings, and the tide rose until it flooded summer homes along the harbor in Edgartown. Everett Allen, in his book *A Wind to Shake the World: The Story of the 1938 Hurricane,* describes water climbing halfway up the eaves of the Edgartown Yacht Club, with the piano afloat inside.

Bessie

THE COW

The demand for the unpasteurized milk by the summer people used all the supply from our four Jersey cows. When one of the cows, Bessie, got sick, it was a major problem.

Bessie was isolated from the herd and put into a separate pasture. Since she still had to be milked twice a day, I volunteered. I had watched Ralph Harding milk many times and thought it looked easy.

The first day I took a halter, a rope, a bucket of grain, a stool, and the milk bucket to Bessie. Then I set to work.

I could hardly get any milk out. By the time I had a half inch in the bucket, I was almost in tears with frustration and with sore thumbs. It seemed like it took weeks before my thumbs stopped hurting and my technique improved.

I thought I would never use that skill again, but during World War II I worked for a time as a courier for the Frontier Nursing Service in the Kentucky Mountains. There were few roads, and my job was to ride on horseback between nursing centers delivering medicines, mail, and other needs. At one of farthest centers, the nurse had injured herself and couldn't milk the cow. If the cow wasn't milked, she would dry up and not produce milk, a hardship for nurses living where all supplies were brought in by horseback.

I volunteered to move to the center and milk the cow. I milked that cow morning and night for six weeks before the nurse could take over. Everyone was impressed with my technique.

Yet on land on Chappy, virtually free of trees and populated with houses built to withstand severe winter gales
and well back from the beach, there was little wind damage.
Several boathouses were either blown away, blown apart, or
blown off their foundations, but most homes were left intact and no one was injured.

The day after the storm, when the wind had calmed
down, my father and Artie went to see what had happened

*After the hurricane the men of the
island try to extract a car upturned
and half-buried in sand.*

in the harbor and to *Gadget*. There was not much left of the dirt road to the ferry, and the ferry house was off its foundation. Several cars were buried in sand, boats from the harbor were thrown up on the beach, and the shoreline on both sides was full of debris.

At first there was no sign of *Gadget*. Then someone on the waterfront in Edgartown said he had spied *Gadget* going out of the harbor during the storm with her bow down and

Buildings were moved or left akimbo on Chappy Point after the hurricane.

stern up, obviously dragging the huge mooring block my father had put down – which some had scoffed at as being "big enough for the *Queen Mary*."

The next morning Artie found an undamaged rowboat, rowed out to *Gadget*, pumped some water out of her and tried the engine. "It started like a kitten purring," he said when he brought her back into the harbor. She was one of the few boats in the harbor that survived. Later reports said at least twenty were flung up on the Chappy shore, on the Edgartown shore, or disappeared toward Hyannis or Falmouth, never to be seen again.

IF THE STORM A FEW YEARS EARLIER HAD LET CHAPPY OFF easily, World War II changed our lives on the island dramatically. Our safe haven, our paradise, had disappeared.

Rationing of gas and some foods meant the trips to Chappy were precarious. We used all our gas rations to get there, which left no more gas except for farm use and an occasional trip to town to get food. We were lucky to have most of our own food, milk from the cows, chickens and turkeys from the barnyard, pork from last year's pig, and all the vegetables and fruit you could want.

As the war intensified, my sisters and I could both sense and see the danger the adults felt. Coast Guardsmen were stationed at the house at Wasque, the one with the tower, and at the keeper's house at the Cape Pogue Lighthouse. They patrolled East Beach 24 hours a day. One guard started at Wasque and walked to the dike, and another started at the other end at Cape Pogue Lighthouse and walked to the dike, checking in at telephone posts along the way, always aware of the fear by the government that the Germans might try to land.

A tall lookout tower was built at Wasque Point at the beginning of the war. The tower had tall legs with a cabin-like shelter on the top. We weren't allowed up, but managed to talk our way to the top just once to see the incredible view.

During the war the Coast Guard had a "telephone crew" during the summer whose assignment was to put in an underground phone line the length of South and East beaches. My father offered to put them up, and ten of them stayed in our Camp, the smallest building on Pimpneymouse. Four double-decker bunks in the back room provided space for half the crew to sleep. The cook slept in a small alcove off the kitchen. The rest must have slept on the screened porch, which had plastic over the screens to keep out the wind and rain.

Coast Guardsmen enjoy a break from putting in a phone line along East Beach.

My father showed them wonderful hospitality, including clambakes, fishing trips, and riding horses. My father's boat, *Gadget*, was a Coast Guard Auxiliary boat, and he had to go out on patrol regularly, but always seemed to carry fishing rods with him. The men of the telephone crew were very much a part of our lives. They put up cut-off telephone poles for our clothesline, which we still use. One of the guardsmen taught my sister Ruthie to climb those poles with spikes on her legs – quite a sight.

Most boats were not allowed in or out of the harbor, but having volunteered for the Coast Guard Auxiliary, my father did frequent patrols. His main job was to watch over the outer harbor on *Gadget*, to keep boats from leaving, and to watch for suspicious boats wanting to come in. However, he found time and a way to take the young Coast Guardsmen water-skiing during his "patrols."

Everyone on the Vineyard was required to have a "waterfront pass" if they went near the water or over on the ferry. No one ever asked to see it, since the police knew all the locals. We used to wander around on East Beach where the Army and Navy were practicing beach landings for the Normandy invasion. Even though we were not supposed to be on the beaches, the soldiers and sailors were delighted to see us and gave us their C-rations.

One day we drove the pony cart down the Dike Road to East Beach, as we had done many times before. We would tie up the pony to a post or the old herring building and go out on the beach to see if anything was going on. Usually there was no one around. This day, for some reason, Babe was spooked and jumpy and didn't want to go. We made her keep going, and I even got out and led her part of the way. She reluctantly completed the journey.

Finding no one around on the beach, we started back up the road. To our astonishment, there were soldiers popping out of "foxholes" all along the road. They had big grins on their faces, delighted that their foxholes had kept them hidden from us, even if not from the pony. I hope it gave them courage when they had to face the real thing on Normandy or Omaha beaches.

The Welch sisters in 1938: from left, Hope, Edo, and Ruth.

Chapter Thirteen

CHANGING CHAPPAQUIDDICK

I F, LIKE RIP VAN WINKLE, I HAD FALLEN ASLEEP IN THE 1930S and awakened in this twenty-first century on Chappaquiddick, I would have been astonished. Instead of an open, sheep-grazed landscape, the now heavily wooded island would have convinced me that I was in the wrong place.

Changes came slowly at first, but increased rapidly after 1973. Pimpneymouse Farm is still here, looking much as it did in the 1930s. A riding ring was added to accommodate horse training when horses replaced the cows, pigs, and chickens. A split rail fence replaced the privet hedge between the driveway and the house. Lightning took down the magnificent flagpole that boasted a swordfish weathervane. The large brass bell that beckoned anyone within earshot and usually at mealtimes has gone. One more house has been built for a caretaker.

Farming is still practiced, but it is now hay, firewood, vegetables, laying hens, and boarding horses. It's my dream that the farming tradition will continue into the fourth generation, even if it is only in a modest way. Times have changed dramatically on Chappy, but a farm could be a valuable source of local food, as it was in the 1930s.

The biggest change on the farm is the condition of the fields and trees. When a farmer stops mowing his fields, cedars and vines appear, then shrubs, and finally pitch pines, cherries, and black and white oaks. A mature tree needs twenty feet distance from its neighbors to reach its full potential. Now, red, white, and black oak trees stand tall against the sky.

Thanksgiving 1938: Babe, Edo, and the homemade canopy on the pony cart.

A vivid reminder of the change in the landscape is illustrated by my memory of a friend named John Silva who flew his small plane into the Trent Field, the long field starting at the paved turn at the Dike Road corner. It was open all the way. John came in over the house at the north end of the field, landed, and taxied up to his father's house across from the present firehouse. Taking off the same way, his route was open and unimpeded by trees or shrubs. Now it is filled with trees, houses, and the fire station.

Immediately after World War II, the outside world had minimal interest in Chappy. Land was of low value, and the summer people were slow to return. The big Victorian house overlooking Katama Bay that had belonged to John J. Jeremiah, a landmark on a small island, was an albatross to most people. When it was offered for sale as the largest house on Chappy, no one was interested in buying it. At its bank auction in 1944, only a few people showed up for the bidding. The opening bid was $4,000, and the winning bid was $5,000. Today, that house is worth millions.

Chappy stayed low key, sparsely settled, and rural until 1969, when Senator Edward "Ted" Kennedy's accident turned the national spotlight onto the island. Suddenly tourists flocked to Chappaquiddick to see the now-famous Dike Bridge and to cut pieces from it as a souvenir. The "party house" and the sharp turn in the road where the wrong turn was made are still tourist attractions.

Tourists and sightseers saw the beauty of East Beach, Poucha Pond, and Wasque Point. Old-timers who had lived on the Vineyard all their lives and boasted that they had never been to Chappaquiddick hurried to see the site of the accident and realized what a special place East Beach was and the good fishing it provided.

INCREASED INTEREST MEANT INCREASED TRANSPORTATION NEEDS. Instead of the one small, slow ferry of the 1930s, now two large ferries ply the channel on a seven-minute ride, fighting the current from the new opening in South

Looking from Chappy Point to Edgartown. The coal wharf is to the left of "Steamboat Dock," now Memorial Wharf.

Beach created in April of 2007. Norton Point, formerly called South Beach, is no longer available to the four-wheel-drive vehicles that used to make their way over it to Chappy.

Now, long lines of cars wait for the ferry. With the ferry schedule now running until midnight in the summer, the pace of life on Chappy has become frenetic in comparison to the lazy days of summer in the 1930s, when people went to town by catboat once a week.

In July of 1954, only seventy-four houses existed on Chappy, most of them summer homes. Now there are

approximately 450. In 1970 there were only thirty year-round residents; now, there are about 150 families.

The year 1954 also marked the beginning of the Chappaquiddick Island Association, whose purpose is to provide information to Chappaquiddick residents and a forum for residents to discuss and settle major issues. Meetings were held in living rooms around the island. It has become a valuable voice for Chappy, when needed, to unite behind a common cause. As assessments soared, waterfront residents used the forum of the Association to protest unfair tax increases. During the 1950s a group of taxpayers and Association members sued the Town for an unreasonable increase in taxes and won the lawsuit.

The Chappy Community Center was a major change to Chappaquiddick, providing a community gathering place. Started in 1988 it was supported by virtually all the residents of Chappy, either by work or by dollars. As the summer and winter population has grown, the value of the Community Center has increased. It provides a place to gather and hold meetings and community gatherings and classes. Summer sailing and tennis classes for the young, yoga classes for adults, movies for all ages, lectures, nature walks, and concerts round out a stimulating summer agenda.

Regular potluck dinners both in winter and summer and hosted by volunteers welcome all residents who appreciate the favorite recipes from island kitchens and the produce from Chappy gardens. A Wednesday afternoon summer farmer's market, begun in 2007, has generated interest in homegrown vegetables and fruits. A July Fair has a variety

A young Hope holds a beagle puppy.

of attractions, such as the popular used book sale, a dog show, and the grilled hot dogs and hamburgers that light up the faces of the hungry.

THE HOUSING BOOM ON CHAPPY STARTED IN EARNEST IN 1973. During my years on the Edgartown Planning Board starting in 1973 and my twelve years as Selectman in Edgartown from 1980 to 1992, I spent many nights returning to

Chappy on the last ferry. With limited ferry service, it was easy to count those who lived here year-round. I discovered that the low point in the number of winter residents occurs during the month of February.

Numbers of year-rounders crept up slowly at first, as did housing starts. Both escalated in the 1980s and 1990s. I stopped counting when the number of year-rounders surpassed 100 people in 1989 and stopped counting new housing construction at the millennium when the yearly figure for house starts was over twenty per year.

A view from the top of the hill beyond the Big Camp, looking south toward Edgartown in the 1930s – a vastly different landscape from now.

The making of the movie *Jaws* in 1974 brought an influx of tourists and had an impact on our lives. For the Potter family, *Jaws* was of particular interest, as our dog Pipit, accompanied by our son Stephen, acted in it. Both were paid for their work as actors. Pipit earned $500. Then copying my father's lesson years ago about supporting charities, I insisted that the money Pipit earned should be donated to the Edgartown branch of the Massachusetts Society for the Prevention of Cruelty to Animals and not go into Stephen's pocket, since he had his own earnings from the movie.

The Welch sisters in 2009, from left, Hope, Edo, and Ruth.

A second stimulus during the 1990s was created by President Clinton and his family spending summers on the Vineyard. This brought more publicity. Tourists who came to the Vineyard to catch a glimpse of the President and his family also wanted to see Chappaquiddick and the famous Dike Bridge.

Surf fishing became increasingly popular with the advent of the rod and reel in the 1940s, and the sport expanded exponentially when beryllium and glass rods supplanted heavy bamboo ones. Spinning reels and four-wheel-drive vehicles appeared after World War II. With the beaches under the supervision of The Trustees of Reservations after 1959, the balance between the protection of birds and wildlife with the needs of the surf casters has been successful. As the beaches on the main island became more crowded, East

Beach, the Cedars, and Wasque represent oases where one can still experience the peace and quiet of the old days.

The dramatic growth and change on Chappy during the last almost eight decades has been ameliorated by the Martha's Vineyard Land Bank. With the help of the Chappy Open Space Committee, Sheriff's Meadow Foundation, and the generosity of Chappy residents, the Land Bank has preserved and opened to the public many of the island's special places. With the Land Bank's extensive trail system, it is possible to walk from Wasque to Cape Pogue Pond, over three miles, and cross a paved road only twice.

The Land Bank has reopened some of the old fields that have grown up into trees and some of the old cart paths that were used by horse and buggy. In my young days, three ruts still showed on some of the old dirt roads. The middle rut was made by the horse and the two outer ruts were made by the cart wheels.

Although we have seen dramatic changes in the landscape, the houses, and the population, Chappaquiddick still retains a quality of life that is not found in many other places on the eastern seaboard. I feel fortunate and privileged to have lived on Chappaquiddick for almost eighty years.

CHANGES HAVE COME TO MY FAMILY, TOO. MY FATHER DIED suddenly in 1945. My mother lived another forty-seven years and returned to her roots in Boston. However, she kept the farm going in a modest way with the help of Ralph Harding,

our long time employee. She returned to Chappy every summer, for all the holidays, and whenever her family was here.

After college all three of her daughters moved away from
Chappaquiddick but carried with them the memories of
growing up here and the things they had done. Hope ended
up living on a working farm in South Carolina, but she and
her family returned to Pimpneymouse Farm every summer.
Her husband, Bud, flew up as much as possible when he
could get away from his farming responsibilities. Ruth, the
oldest, moved to Switzerland after graduating from Vassar
College having majored in French. First she worked with a
photographer and later became involved in a Swiss, French,
and Protestant publishing house for many years, overseeing
the production of each publication.

Bob and I and our four children lived in Cambridge,
Princeton, and Providence. However, we came to Chappy
every chance we could get, for long summers and every
vacation. With all the moving in our lives, Chappy seemed
like home to us. In 1970 Bob, a professor, had a sabbatical
from Brown University and chose to spend it working on
Chappy. I was at first reluctant to live here year-round. There
were only thirty families living on the island, and I thought
it might be lonely.

After one year, I was hooked and didn't want to return to
the city. The next winter I volunteered to rewrite the zoning
bylaw for Chappaquiddick, creating three-acre lots instead of
one-acre lots. When it was welcomed by the Planning Board
and voted at Town meeting, my future path was clear and I
found myself immersed in Edgartown's governance.

The next generation helped restart the farm, and has remained involved with the farm and the island. Our son, Stephen, majored in agricultural economics in college, and he created and ran Seaside Dairy in Edgartown for five years. During that time, he helped us with Pimpneymouse Farm.

My daughter, Harriett "Hatsy" Potter, lives on the farm and has helped chronicle the history of Chappaquiddick in the book she edited, *Chappaquiddick: That Sometimes Separated but Never Equaled Island,* which was published in 2008 by the Chappaquiddick Island Association and has helped preserve so many of the old stories of Chappy.

Our oldest daughter Priscilla, called Sandy, has turned parts of the farm into an arboretum. It has become well known, and one recent summer sixty members of the Garden Club of America came to see it.

Our middle daughter, Kathy, lives the closest, in Scituate, Massachusetts, and she and her family are here frequently year-round to help on the farm. Her two children were deck hands on the Chappy ferry for a number of years, and Kathy comes to help with the farm.

MANY OF TODAY'S RESIDENTS HAVE A PASSION FOR THE ISLAND, shown by their generosity in helping to save land for future generations to enjoy.

Yet the ferry *On Time III* is under increasing pressure to serve the needs of islanders and visitors. The Chappy ferry is both a blessing and a problem. Personally, I believe the ferry is an asset to Chappy. The wait in line on the Chappy side is one of the best parts of my day. Watching the sun-spangled water, the gray storm waves, the changing sky, the wind on the water, the clouds, the boating activities, and the struggles of the ferry against the current is always fascinating to me. For me it is a welcome time to relax, take stock, to read, to write, or to catch up on my needlepoint.

Whether you board by car or on foot, the ferry is where you see your friends and neighbors, where you catch up on the news, the weather, and the gossip. On shore, you watch joyous reunions between families and friends and happy gatherings preparing for a day on the beach. It's fascinating to watch the marsh hawk sliding low over the marsh and dune grass, tilting from side to side as he searches the grasses and shrubs next to the car for mice and voles. He floats sharply upward with little effort until he sees his prey when, in one swoop, he grabs it. Gulls drop their shellfish on the pavement nearby, to crack them open and have a feast.

How lucky we are to live in a place where we have a chance each day to talk to neighbors, friends, business people, fishermen, and the eclectic group of people who ride the Chappy ferry. How lucky we are to be able to watch the evolving scene, the water, and wildlife close by.

WHAT DOES THE FUTURE HOLD FOR THE MULTIGENERA-tional Pimpneymouse Farm? That will depend upon the decisions made by the third and fourth generations of the family, when my generation is gone. At that point eight family members will inherit the farm. With disparate interests, the eight will have some tough decisions to make.

What do I wish? Of course, I wish that everything could remain the same. In this world that is unlikely. However, the increasing cost of the ferry, the congestion, and traffic problems on both sides may prove self-limiting to newcomers. Individuals will decide whether they are willing to tolerate the obstacles that face them if they move to Chappaquiddick.

In the meantime, the third generation on the farm hopes to keep the farm going, so that the next generations will have a choice and an opportunity to preserve the land as a farm if that is their wish.

Taking a broader look at Chappy as a whole, I believe and hope that the landowners, renters, and visitors to this island will continue to cherish this bit of land, its rural qualities, its waters, both salt and fresh, its beaches, its woods, its fields and wetlands and its vistas. Surrounded as it is by Nantucket Sound, Muskeget Channel, Katama Bay, and Edgartown Harbor, it is a very special corner of the world, worth preserving for future generations.

Acknowledgments

THE IDEA FOR THIS BOOK WAS BORN IN THE MID-1990s when Ralph Graves asked me to write a story about Chappaquiddick for a book he and painter Ray Ellis were working on called *Martha's Vineyard: An Affectionate Memoir.* I discovered it was fun to reminisce at the computer and his editing was remarkable and encouraging.

I muddled along until 2006 when a notice in an Edgartown Council of Aging newsletter announced a Writer's Workshop. I realized that if I was ever going to accomplish my goal of writing down my memories of early Chappy, I should sign up for the workshop. Elaine Pace was a wonderful teacher, and after the workshop, I continued to work with her. Elaine introduced me to Jan Pogue of Vineyard Stories. That has been a wonderful experience and made me appreciate what a good editor and publisher can do.

The photographs were taken by my father, Charles A. Welch, between 1929 and 1938, and by my sister Ruth

Welch until 1946. They provide a visual history of the farm and the island.

My husband Bob cooked dinners so that I had time to sit at the computer in the late afternoons. My daughter Kathy Miller was a great help with wording, punctuation, clarity, and constructive criticism. Daughter Hatsy inspired me with her book on Chappaquiddick. She also helped me with my minimal computer skills, as well as helping to edit the manuscript.

Both sisters, Ruth and Hope, were good critics with helpful suggestions, especially when my memory of the "old days" failed. My sister-in-law Hope Hickock helped me understand what was needed to clarify parts of the book for readers unfamiliar with Chappaquiddick.

Nis Kildegaard bailed me out of a number of problems with the computer. He was always available by phone, or by making "house calls" on his bicycle when I got seriously stuck. He also helped me with the old photos.

Dana Gaines skillfully improved the map of Chappaquiddick, and the enthusiastic support of Tom Dunlop has been important to me.

Without all this help and encouragement, this book would never have been published.